Healing Body, Self and Soul

Integrative Somatic Psychotherapy

Jerry Perlmutter, PhD

BALBOA
PRESS
A DIVISION OF HAY HOUSE

Copyright © 2015 Jerry Perlmutter, PhD.

All rights reserved. No part of this book may be used or reproduced by any means, graphic, electronic, or mechanical, including photocopying, recording, taping or by any information storage retrieval system without the written permission of the publisher except in the case of brief quotations embodied in critical articles and reviews.

Balboa Press books may be ordered through booksellers or by contacting:

Balboa Press
A Division of Hay House
1663 Liberty Drive
Bloomington, IN 47403
www.balboapress.com
1 (877) 407-4847

Because of the dynamic nature of the Internet, any web addresses or links contained in this book may have changed since publication and may no longer be valid. The views expressed in this work are solely those of the author and do not necessarily reflect the views of the publisher, and the publisher hereby disclaims any responsibility for them.

The author of this book does not dispense medical advice or prescribe the use of any technique as a form of treatment for physical, emotional, or medical problems without the advice of a physician, either directly or indirectly. The intent of the author is only to offer information of a general nature to help you in your quest for emotional and spiritual well-being. In the event you use any of the information in this book for yourself, which is your constitutional right, the author and the publisher assume no responsibility for your actions.

Any people depicted in stock imagery provided by Thinkstock are models, and such images are being used for illustrative purposes only.
Certain stock imagery © Thinkstock.

Print information available on the last page.

Library of Congress Control Number: 2015910112

ISBN: 978-1-5043-3592-8 (sc)
ISBN: 978-1-5043-3591-1 (hc)
ISBN: 978-1-5043-3593-5 (e)

Balboa Press rev. date: 09/18/2015

CONTENTS

Preface xi
    Acknowledgements.. xi

Introduction xv
    Who I Am Professionally xv
    A Brief History of My Becoming a Body Psychotherapist xvi
    My Approach to Psychotherapy xviii
    Defining ISP: The Sources of the Name, Integrative Somatic
    Psychotherapy xxii
        Integrative xxii
        Somatic xxiii
        Psychotherapy... xxiii

Chapter 1 ISP's Guiding Assumptions, Concepts and Values. 1
    Basic Assumptions... 1
    The Therapeutic Relationship 2
    ISP is Holistic 5
    Energy Phenomena... 8
    Armoring 9
    Exercise Interventions.. 11
        Illustration 1. The Sensing Position........................... 12
        Illustration 2. The Backward Bow and the Forward
        Arch 13

Illustration 3. The Side-to-Side Movement and Stress Position 15

Chapter 2 ISP's Core Treatment Processes 17
The Awareness Cycle 19
Paradoxical Change 21
An Introduction to the Exploration of the Soul and Spirit ... 22

Chapter 3 ISP and the Treatment of Character 24
Traumas Shape Character 24
The Psychoanalytic Perspective of Character Formation 26
Using Character to Further Structure ISP Treatment 28
Healing Trauma to Reduce Character Strictures 30
Some Further Clarity about the Use of Character in ISP 32
Some Cautions Before We Proceed 32
   Character Nomenclature 32
   The Complexity of Character Types 33
   Healing Character by Externalizing Introjects 34
   Another Caution Before We Deal with Character Based Psychotherapy 34
   Why Use Character Types in this Book? 34
   The Structure of the Character Treatment Sections that Follow 35
   A Practicality 35

Chapter 4 Treating the Oral Character 36
Etiology 36
Somatic Aspects of the Oral 37
Treatment of the Oral 38
   The Injustice of the Lack of Nurturance 40
   Working Out the Feelings of Past Anger and Pain 40
   Sequencing Anger and Pain Work 40
   The Use of Specific Body Interventions 41
      Illustration 4. Leveling the Back 41

  Illustration 5. Heart to Heart................................ 43
 Self-Nurturing Skills. 45
  Patient's Narrative.. 46

Chapter 5 Treating the Anal Masochist................................ 60
 Etiology.. 60
 Somatic Aspects of the Masochist.............................. 61
  Face, Neck and Shoulder Girdle 61
  Pelvic Girdle 62
  Legs... 62
 The Therapy of the Masochist 63
  Illustration 6. Ironing the Chest 64
  Illustration 7. Holding His Heart Between Her Hands 65
  A Therapist's Narrative of Psychotherapy
  with an Anal Masochist by Leighton Clark,
  Psychotherapist 67

Chapter 6 The Treatment of the Schizoid 75
 Etiology.. 75
 Schizoid Body Structure... 76
  The Head... 76
  Splitting of the Head from the Body..................... 76
  The Body 76
  Breathing.. 77
  Legs.. 77
 The Therapy of the Schizoid 78
  Overriding Issues.. 78
  Treatment Interventions 78
   Illustration 8. The Eye Opener........................... 80
   Illustration 9. Eye Comfort 81
 A Schizoid Patient's Treatment Narrative 82
 Entry Issues 83
 Dual Relationships 86

Chapter 7 Treatment of the Phallic Hysteric 100
Etiology.. 100
Hysteric Body Structure 101
    Bottom Half of the Body...101
    Upper Half of the Body.. 102
The Treatment of the Hysteric... 102
    The Use of Exercises 102
    The Use of Touch Work...103
        Illustration 10. Greasing the Pelvic Hinge 105
        Illustration 11. Resting the Pelvic Hinge 106

Chapter 8 The Treatment of the Phallic Narcissist.............. 108
Etiology.. 108
Phallic-Narcissistic Body Structure......................................110
The Therapy of the Narcissist 112
    Illustration 12. Loosening the Diaphragm....................114
    Illustration 13. The Easy Chair......................................117
    A Summary of the Strategy of Healing the Phallic
    Narcissist 118
        A Phallic Narcissistic Patient's Testimony............ 118
Wrapping up Character and Body Therapy 129
    Patients Primarily Determine When to Terminate
    ISP 129
    ISP and the Process of Transformative Change........... 130

Chapter 9 Identifying More Healing Interventions Of
                Integrative Somatic Psychotherapy..................... 132
Introduction... 132
Concretizing Metaphors 132
    A Patient Narrative of Concretizing a Metaphor 133
    Another Patient's Narrative of Concretizing a
    Metaphor... 134
Dreaming While Awake... 139
The Stages of ISP..141

  Illustration 14. The Two Stages of ISP 142

Chapter 10 Moving Towards the End of the Psychotherapy. 144
 Introduction 144
 Forgiveness 145
  Illustration 15. A Matrix of Forgiveness 146
  A Patient Narrative of Forgiveness 147
 Gratitude 150
  Patient Narrative about Gratitude 153
  Another Patient Narrative about Gratitude 153
 Terminating Psychotherapy 154
 My Termination with this Book 158

Bibliography 161

Jerry Perlmutter, PhD, Professional Activities 165

PREFACE

Acknowledgements

I would like to acknowledge some of the people who played important roles in my professional development.

John Collier, anthropology professor at the City College of New York, taught me reverence and respect for the ways of all people, all cultures.

Clark Moustakos at the Merrill-Palmer Institute in Detroit was my first client-centered psychotherapy supervisor as I worked with children. I later had client-centered teachers at the house that Carl Rogers built, the University of Chicago's Counseling & Psychotherapy Center, where I took coursework in conducting psychotherapy and more supervision as I worked with children. From both of these experiences I learned to be empathic, and to respect my patients' capacities to participate in their own healing and development.

Jerry Perlmutter, PhD

Carl Whitaker, Professor at the University of Wisconsin, modeled utilizing all of self as a psychotherapist, letting go of depending on theory, and floating on a raft of informed intuition.

I am in debt to the NTL Institute for Applied Behavioral Science. There I learned to move from theory to practice fluidly, effectively and congruently.

I am also in debt to Alan Richardson, who gave me my initial training in body psychotherapy. He was trained by Malcolm Brown, who at that time was more committed to body psychotherapy, as defined by Wilhelm Reich and Alexander Lowen.

I appreciate those who worked as staff with me over the thirty-six years that we did Soul Workshops, one-week workshops, which incorporated bodywork (soft and deep tissue massage), exercise, spontaneous expressive movement, art, yoga and meditation. These workshops were used as less expensive ways to do therapy intensives, and they were very rich and deep experiences for participants. The staff included Joyce Weir, Murry Perlmutter, Marianne Johnson, Leighton Clark and Barbara Cargill.

Persons connected to the Midwest Institute for Somatic Psychotherapy in Illinois have given me support in the development of Integrative Somatic Psychotherapy over the years, especially: Leighton Clark, Bonnie Summers, Larry Carroll, Jeannie Kokes, Carole Veronesi, Christie Ahrens, Bridget Penney, Nancy Voss, Steve Treacy and Carolyn Faivre. They were Board Members of this non-profit professional organization.

To my professional colleagues: Leighton Clark, Marianne Johnson, Bill Waldner, Phil Metres and Darrell Nicks, I give them my thanks for their help.

Healing Body, Self and Soul

To two key persons who helped me to generate this book with the quality it has: the artist, Scott Wills, who developed the cover of the book and all of its illustrations; to Mitchell Kupferberg who edited the manuscript.

I appreciate the patients I have accompanied on courageous journeys of self-discovery and transformation over 41 years. We have learned from each other.

INTRODUCTION

Who I Am Professionally

I have been a teacher or a trainer all of my adult life. I started at age 18 when I taught new employees how to convert gas refrigerators so that they used natural gas instead of the older bottle gas. I have gone on to teach professionals in all kinds of settings.

In an organizational change context, I have trained managers and line workers. I have trained boards of non-profit organizations. I have taught nurses, social workers and psychologists to do group psychotherapy. I have taught group and consulting skills to psychologists, social workers and business school graduate students. These constitute only a sample of my training work.

I have received excellent body psychotherapy treatment from Malcolm and Kathryn Brown. I have been inspired by the writings of Alexander Lowen from the start of my career. My experiences giving and receiving body psychotherapy have led me to develop my own ways of working in this modality. I have been asked to train body psychotherapists, and this was pivotal in leading me to write and document my approach. In order to teach, I had to make explicit what I had been doing implicitly and intuitively, so that I could communicate this to trainees.

For more than thirty years I have used systems theory[*] in my Organizational Development practice.

All of my conceptualization about individuals, groups and organizations entail the fundamental use of the systems approach. When I started to practice, the systems approach entailed how work organizations transform information to create value. Body psychotherapy has led me to expand my view of systems in that they also *transform energy*, and this too is crucial to the quality of their functioning and to the quality of their outputs. This latter approach has expanded my knowledge of humanity and enormously increased the ways in which I intervene when I do body psychotherapy.

A Brief History of My Becoming a Body Psychotherapist

Immediately, it comes to me that I want to briefly report the full swath of the development of this manuscript. I am drawn into sharing from my starting as a patient in body psychotherapy. A colleague of mine, for whom I felt a lot of respect, suddenly announced to me that he had started receiving body psychotherapy and really liked it. On the spot, I decided that I would try it, too. And, from the start,

---

[*] To be explicit about systems theory, I am using the notion of the interdependence among units or subsystems of the larger system, which is the whole person here. Intervening in one subsystem, such as loosening the ring of chronic muscle tightness at the base of the skull with deep touch, will affect all of the other subsystems of the person, e.g. the increased blood flow to the brain may deepen thinking, intensify feeling, foment actions and may become more spontaneous. The person will become more animated.

it felt right for me too; I had a gut feeling of it being a good fit for me. This is not a reflection that the therapy was fun, entertaining or a romp. I did work on painful, traumatic experiences and events that provoked my anger and rage. But working on these events felt right to me; I had to do this to reach for my authentic self. I wanted this connection very much.

After a few years of work, my therapist told me he was starting a training group, and he invited me to join. I was enthralled with taking the training. I developed a physical exercise program for myself, to help me do the work well. Then I made a decision to stay in body therapy for years, till I had certainty that I had worked myself as much as I could. I owed this to my future patients so that I did not lay my personal (unfinished) issues on them. I was in therapy for nine to ten years. My first therapist was a male. And then I had therapy with a woman. I also had an intensive with a married couple. Each of these therapist situations helped me to work different areas of my life. I also attended a training workshop with Alexander Lowen and had some therapy sessions with him while I was on a sabbatical from my teaching position. I attended training sessions with well-known body therapists whenever I could. For example, I invited Ron Kurtz to take over a session of the training group that I attended, with our trainer's approval.

It became obvious to me that I was starting to work psychotherapeutically with patients differently than any of the body therapists that I got therapy from or trained with. I noticed this and then went on to name what I was practicing, Integrative Somatic Psychotherapy (ISP), because it captured my style of working.

About twenty or more years ago several people asked me to do a workshop presenting my form of psychotherapy. I started with a weekend, and they wanted more. So I led a series of sessions. Then the group asked for a year of workshops. As we approached the end of this year, many of them decided to be trained to be ISP practitioners. I thought it would take three years of 27 spaced sessions. They agreed to join me. Then we decided there would be supervision of their work with their initial patients. And this program led to a certificate from the Midwest Institute for Somatic Psychotherapy, a non-profit professional organization that I helped to found in order to establish and promote ISP. Teaching ISP required me to be explicit about much of my treatment work since so much of it was developed using my intuition. This explication of ISP for training others is one foundation of this book.

My Approach to Psychotherapy

I am very much influenced by the client-centered approach. I have learned to be empathic and more accepting and respectful of my patients' perceptions, assumptions, feelings, and values. I also have organized my own psychotherapy efforts so that the self-actualization of the patient is maximized in ISP too. Importantly, I have restated and extended this proposition as follows: all of the resources that patients need to heal and grow exist inside them; the key role of psychotherapy is to help patients to gain fuller access to these inner resources so that they can integrate them into their lives. Patients benefit greatly from developing these newly discovered resources.

I have learned to increasingly allow the psychotherapy to spontaneously unfold. I do not have to control many of the events of a treatment session for healing to occur. A psychotherapy process that is heavily influenced by the patient's spontaneity yields surprising (to me and to my patients) avenues of healing and growth.

Another important aspect of my role as therapist is to *stimulate* the patient in ways that increasingly reveal to them their inner resources. I stimulate a patient to be aware of their inner resources and then it is up to the patient to use what emerges in their unique way for their benefit.

This emphasis on stimulation takes me beyond the client-centered approach. As I use body psychotherapy in this way, I refer to stimulating situations as "opportunities" (I use this term in psychotherapy and in body workshops). In a treatment session opportunities became *new experiences* that I help to stimulate, or that patients discover and use for themselves.

Self-discovered, new experiences require an environment that is safe and supportive to the patient. For example, I had a patient who spontaneously started moving in a standing position. I encouraged her to let her body explore this movement further. She started lumbering around the room stomping her feet. She came in touch with a gorilla aspect of her. She explored this part of herself more fully. I supported her living in the gorilla part of her during her session and then also in her outside life, when this was possible. This gorilla part emerged from a woman who had not felt very powerful and also has kept very tight control over her behavior. This gorilla experience is transforming for her. As a result of living deeply in the gorilla part of her, she has become more gentle, flowing and graceful in her personal life and work.

I am most interested in the *behavioral change* of patients with whom I work. Increasing awareness and insights are useful, but ultimately I support individuals to increase their repertoire of behavior. I also strive to help persons to live lives that reflect, or are congruent, with their core selves and their souls. In this way their lives become more meaningful, inspired and energized. To me this is one of the more important aspects of psychotherapeutic success.

In summary, these are some of the key psychotherapeutic aspects of the writing that follows: Helping patients to gain a fuller access to their inner resources; and providing stimulation so that patients go more deeply and broadly into themselves to find inner resources that previously they did not know they possessed.

Integrating energy phenomena into systems theory has opened me up to a set of viewpoints that have been very useful and expansive in understanding and treating individuals. Body structures and physiological functions are energy incarnate. One can intervene to alter the structure and the physical functioning of the body, and the pattern of body energy will be significantly altered. In turn, psychological interventions alter body processes and the flow of energy.

Advances on all these levels influence the spiritual development of the individual. In turn, spiritual deepening of the individual has profound influences on psychological and physiological functioning. Therefore, one can enter any of the different sub-systems of the individual's multiple levels. *It is best to initiate interventions at the level that is most obvious and conscious to the patient.* To me, this is an exciting and useful perspective. Importantly, introducing change at any one of these levels may foster deep, sweeping change at all levels of the system of the organism.

When nothing specific becomes obvious or conscious to the patient, I favor doing body interventions: spontaneous movement, exercises, and especially deep touch. I favor deep touch because it is highly efficient in mobilizing the patient. In deep touch I often use my thumbs sometimes my elbows to apply deep pressure on muscles. Sometimes the deep touch is swept along the length of the muscle. *I use what I see or feel in the patient to direct me where to do touch work.*

After a patient responds to a specific intervention, then the therapist can help expand the effectiveness of this stimulation by acting on other levels of their system. For example, deep touch to the neck

Healing Body, Self and Soul

may open up the flow of energy to the arms (identified in the report of the patient or by visible vibrations in their arm muscles). Then the therapist can ask the patient to raise their arms (if the patient is supine), and to allow their arms *to move the way they want to*, while they pay attention to what they experience. I have had patients spontaneously erupt into powerful movements of pushing away a pillow I hold, that they envision as a past perpetrator whom they were too weak to resist when they were traumatized at an early age. Or after helping patients to express angry feelings by responding empathically to them, their jaw muscles may start vibrating, or their retracted jaw becomes positioned more forward.

Another way I work is to become a cheerleader who supports intensifying whatever the patient is experiencing and expressing. Often the initial feelings that flow out when armor is being reduced is quite contained. It can be a wonderful and freeing and healing experience to let go and express oneself more fully. An example of cheerleading behavior is in responding to a patient's initial emotional expressions by empathic statements with more emotional intensity than the patient allowed herself. Often, as a result, the patient starts expressing stronger feelings. Or I may repeat what they are saying; only I simply say it more loudly.

I also facilitate this freeing up by indicating to patients that they can express any feeling and any action, as long as they do not injure themselves or me, and as long as they do not destroy my office. I can even allow destruction if they are willing and able to pay for repairs. And this has happened in the therapy I have done.

Notice that all of the work of the therapist I have described in this section involves using different processes, e.g., deep and soft touches to muscles, expanding on the patient's spontaneous movements, cheerleading emerging feelings, etc. The manner in which I have intervened has evolved significantly over time from a more analytical and deductive way of operating to a more intuitive and inductive way of working with patients. I started out by looking for character structures in a patient, and expanding the exploration of the dimensions of their character. These character structures were defined by Wilhelm Reich (1972) and reaffirmed by Alexander Lowen (1958). As I developed my way of working, I increasingly turned to responding to the experiences of patients; helping them to explore their experiences by introducing process interventions rather than working with content in order to seek out the aspects of character they had not yet experienced nor have not yet become aware of in the therapy. Now I intervene physically moving from head towards the tail; this is the sequence of body development when the child is in the womb and also after birth.

Defining ISP: The Sources of the Name, Integrative Somatic Psychotherapy

Integrative

It is called integrative because numerous concepts and interventions (e.g., from hypnotherapy, psychoanalysis, inner child work and expressive movement) that are not directly related to each other are used in an amalgamated manner. Usually, the original versions are altered so that they meet ISP's psychotherapeutic principles. An example of this modification involves Perl's use of two chairs to explore splits in the client's ego (Perls, 1992, pp.157-163). For example, the client is first asked to talk to her father and then to talk from her father back to herself. The person is asked to hold a dialog between these two parts of herself. Perl's goal was often to increase the integration between the splits in the patient's ego. In ISP, the therapist makes a determination whether the two "ego" states are *native* to the person. If one isn't native, likely the father here, the patient is asked to talk to her father out there. She is asked to see her father in her mind's eye facing her on a mattress propped against an opposite wall. First, she might talk from herself to her father. As she talks to her father she is told she can touch her father in any way that feels right. *She does not talk as her father.*

The goal of this intervention is to externalize the internalized (or introjected) father. This is an important healing step in ISP. As the client does this, he owns himself more fully, more clearly, and more deeply: he becomes more autonomous.

Somatic

It is somatic because it focuses on bodily events and processes that are important in shaping the individual's mind and soul. Many different types of interventions that are utilized are somatic in nature, i.e., touch work, exercises, and spontaneous movement.

Psychotherapy

It is called psychotherapy because it uses verbal interventions from a psychological treatment approach. ISP goes back and forth in a pattern of intervening somatically and then psychologically. The body experiences that emerge from the somatic interventions are dealt with verbally and cognitively to integrate new awareness, new experience of the deeper self and to foster behavior that is congruent with the deeper self.

CHAPTER 1

ISP's Guiding Assumptions, Concepts and Values

Basic Assumptions

The most fundamental assumption of ISP is that people have all the resources they need to heal and grow. The major issue that individuals face is gaining fuller access to their potential. The development of character structure leads to a limiting of resources that are available to the individual. ISP focuses on this important task of expanding access to a person's broader potential.

Opportunities are supported, created or sometimes given to patients to help them make fuller contact with their resources. First, the person's attention is expanded to include their body sensations. In addition, their breath is deepened, raising their consciousness of their inner experiences. Touch work elicits patient experiences that are often related to early traumas. Spontaneous movement is elicited and supported, which often surfaces deeper aspects of the self, new ways of looking at their experience, and new behavioral capabilities. Dream work deepens self-perception and opens persons up to novel perspectives about themselves. These are some examples of how ISP enhances access to inner resources.

The Therapeutic Relationship

This is a complex area in body psychotherapy. We can only cover some of the highlights in this overview.

The therapist usually intervenes early in sessions to increase the energy level and self-awareness of the patient. This enables the patient to play an important part in structuring their session and, ultimately, the course of their psychotherapy.

The ISP therapist responds empathically to the here-and-now experience of the patient. The therapist also helps to deepen this experience by fostering a fuller awareness of the experience as well as the greater meaning that the experience has for the patient. Often, for example, experiences that occur together do so because the patient sees their meanings as related to each other. The therapist deepens the self-awareness of character by stimulating her patient by using touch work, the expansion of spontaneous movement etc. She helps the patient to identify the basic themes that these experiences reflect, the recurring assumptions they are based upon, their etiology, and the basic somatic underpinnings of these experiences.

Thus the therapist supports the patient to look at the pattern of the experiences the patient has been exploring. This helps the patient to develop broader perspectives of herself. This additive process of connecting experiences into patterns is called *induction*; this is the primary approach of ISP.

In contrast to the inductive approach, the use of character theory to intervene to elucidate other aspects of a character that have not emerged yet is called *deduction*. Character theory connects overt behavior with implicit processes that occur in the unconscious. The theory of character types prepares the therapist to look for the other aspects of the character that are not yet conscious to the patient, and character theory is used to structure interventions to make the unconscious process conscious. Using theory to link conscious behavior with unconscious events is referred as *deduction* (vs. induction). Here the therapist uses theory to determine the course of the therapy. This is more the psychoanalytic approach.

Another important facet of the relationship is the establishment of an extremely safe treatment space in its spatial and psychological aspects. The former includes a physically safe environment for the patient to actively express intense emotions without harming himself or the therapist. Mattresses and cushions are deployed to make the office safer. Rugs have a deep, soft cushioning underneath. Sound insulation is used on the walls, doors and ceiling. White sound may be used to mask the patient's sounds. The person can make as much sound as needed without being concerned about being overheard or disturbing others.

As I mentioned previously, *psychologically* the therapist supports the patient to express *any* fantasy, feeling, thought or action short of harming himself, the therapist or destroying office equipment. It is important to implement these limits because they parallel limits that often occur outside the therapy relationships in life's situations. And effective psychotherapy is a process that helps patients to deal more with the realities of their world. At the same time, the patient's thoughts, feelings and actions are accepted without judgment (and with support) by the therapist. This great degree of freedom of expression is crucial to the conduct of ISP.

The therapeutic relationship I am describing can be an extremely challenging one for a therapist to foster and sustain. At times, the emotional, mental, spiritual, and even physical demands on the therapist can be significant. It is essential that psychotherapists practicing ISP develop trust in themselves and courage. Psychotherapists develop *self-trust* and *courage*, by engaging in their own personal ISP psychotherapy, in order to support a patient's fullest expression of their self.

The concept of the holding environment was applied to describing what the psychoanalyst seeks to achieve in the psychotherapeutic setting[*]. The analyst approximates the mother's holding by paying close attention to the patients' experiences, needs, feelings much as a mother does to her infant child. The analyst may also help the patient to arrive at their own insights or meanings for their experiences. The patient's dreams, fantasies, wishes and intense feelings are accepted and the therapist supports the patient's deeper exploration. The analyst also responds with empathy to these patient expressions.

All of these relational statements refer to ways in which the psychoanalyst may *symbolically* create a *holding environment* during a treatment session. This environment supports the patient in regressing back to earlier times in his life when he encountered trauma and his psychosocial development was not yet very established. This regression provides the patient with an opportunity to have corrective emotional experiences and to more fully integrate these earlier events into his psyche.

---

[*] Winnicott (1965) made a basic and important contribution to understanding and improving the psychotherapeutic relationship when he focused on the *holding environment*. Initially he used this phrase to describe and identify a characteristic of effective care-giving relationships between mother and child. Effective mothering involves physically holding infants securely so that children feel safely enveloped. This safety enables infants to risk initiating "stretching behaviors" that are fundamental to their maturation and development. This eventuates in children's development of strong and resilient egos so that they can meet and deal with the "difficulties of life".

ISP uses all of these symbolic ways of creating a holding environment much as a psychoanalyst may do. Importantly, as ISP therapists, we also provide *direct soft touch and containing touch* to patients with our hands and bodies where this early bonding with the mother was insufficient. This type of intervention is extremely healing because it is a very powerful, concrete way of providing a corrective emotional experience!

__ISP is Holistic__

Human experience can be separated conceptually into two major aspects, the somatic and the psychological. This analytic separation is useful because using both viewpoints helps us to formulate a broader range of interventions. This increases the power of the psychotherapy. In contrast, traditional psychotherapy deals mostly with the psychological.

Reich (1949) wrote: "…Language as well as the perception of other's behavior renders the respective physiological state unconsciously, not only figuratively, but in an immediate manner". For example, analytic experience shows that if somebody is called "inaccessible" and "hard," he is also muscularly hypertonic or armored. If patients feel themselves to be "slimy" or "dirty," analysis shows that their character contains major anal elements.

A therapist can generate body interventions that are simple and very effective. One person I dealt with had a dropped shoulder. I asked him to breathe deeply and to exaggerate this drop in his shoulder. He became aware that he was holding himself back from developing his life fully. Then I had him exaggerate his rounded shoulders. As he exaggerated his rounded shoulders, he got into deep mourning of the death of a very close family member. His incomplete mourning was holding him back in his life. I had him see his family member, and talk out-loud about what he needs to say to him. Notice how simple these interventions are, and how productive they can be for the person. This sequence also demonstrates that somatic events can be the embodiment of psychological processes.

The co-occurrence of the somatic and psychological takes place in fundamental and dynamically important ways. Thus, a person who has developed an assumption that the world is an unsafe place and that she is likely to be attacked unpredictably (especially from behind) may protectively develop massive chronic tension in her back muscles.

As the above example shows, assumptions are built into the structure of the body. People who feel burdened may develop shoulders that are very tight and are held high to "shoulder their load". This body characteristic can be used to further the therapist's diagnostic understanding of the patient.

The therapist can also use somatic interventions to directly help the patient to become aware of these issues and to explore them in depth. The ISP practitioner uses deep touch that is hard and then soft to the muscles of the shoulders and neck to start releasing their armoring. Body psychotherapists pay attention to occurrences at the psychological and somatic levels and move back and forth fluidly to intervene at both levels.

For example, I have had patients whose lower jaw is thrust forward. This often signals willfulness and a determination that is very often exercised even when it is unneeded and inappropriate. This is an example of how character gives rise to inflexible behavior. I used deep pressure on the jaw muscles' spasticity to soften them. As these muscles softened, forgotten earlier experiences and attendant emotions frequently came into patients' consciousness. I promoted a full expression of these dammed up feelings and then I supported an identification of the existential issues embedded in these experiences.

Healing Body, Self and Soul

The patient benefits in a major way when she becomes aware of her rigid exercising of excessive, willful determination. I use the loosening of the jaw muscles as one benchmark for the progress of this work.

Similarly, I had a middle-aged male patient who already showed primarily masochistic and oral aspects. His name was Steve*. One prominent body symptom was that he had recurring sciatica. No Chiropractic treatment had been fully successful. The symptoms abated and then got intense again. During a session, I had Steve pay attention to his inner experience and breathe deeply. Then I asked him to experiment with moving his body in ways that felt right and to continue to breathe deeply. (I started with a minimally structured intervention, knowing that if nothing significant emerged, I could follow-up by asking him to explore movement in his pelvis.)

I asked Steve to notice what he experienced as he moved. He ended up rolling his pelvis in a circle repeatedly. Steve had an image emerge of the inside of his pelvis being a garage that was unfinished on the inside (it had no wallboard).

During the next several sessions Steve returned to this movement and to this unfinished garage image. First, he realized it had to do with his father leaving his mother and abandoning him at the age of one. This thought emerged suddenly. His father had no further contact with Steve after he left. In this session and subsequent ones, Steve got into intense feelings and expressed anger and rage at his father for abandoning him. He saw his father on the mattress before him and beat him on the mattress until he was exhausted. After several sessions of expressing his anger, he suddenly shifted to mourning his father's leaving. He had deep feelings of sadness. After this part of his therapy, Steve's sciatic pain disappeared and did not recur during the course of his psychotherapy and beyond.

* Pseudonyms are used for all characters

Energy Phenomena

Reich identified a crucial aspect of the person—*bioenergy*—that is highly useful in mind-body work. Bioenergy is a longitudinal flow of energy, which moves from the front of the pelvis, up towards the head and then down from the back of the head to the back of the pelvis. This energy also moves from the front of the pelvis down towards the feet, and then returns to the pelvis via the backs of the legs. When the energy flows in the front of the trunk, softer feelings like love, trust and fear are experienced. By contrast, the flow of energy in the back of the body involves harder feelings of anger and aggression.

Bioenergy is a crucial concept that has a dual occurrence at both somatic and psychological levels. As a body process, it involves movement of energy both at the surface of the body and more deeply at the level of blood flow and nerve conduction. (Nerves are closely associated physiologically with the vascular system. During embryonic life, nerves grow along the "lanes" created by blood vessels, assuring nerves of the plentiful supply of blood that they need to function.)

The psychological aspect of this energy flow as it intensifies, is the experience of feeling more emotionally alive, animated, resolute, active and engaged. This energy is more accurately named *psychobiological energy*, and I will refer to it as such in this book.

This increased freedom of energy flow and heightened vitality is supported by the looseness of attendant muscles (versus the chronic spasticity of these muscles, which choke off the energy flow). In addition, the person's level of metabolism is affected by the fullness of breathing so that the oxygenation of the blood and body tissue is maximal. All these aforementioned factors suggest specific body interventions that can be used to increase energy, if this is needed. For example, I have helped patients increase the vital capacity of their breathing by placing my hands on their ribs and pushing as they exhale while they are in a supine position (more about this later). As their rib cage opens up and their breath deepens, their energy level increases markedly, and their ability to recover unconscious memories is enhanced.

Armoring

Threatening situations trigger people to defend their integrity by mobilizing their ego mechanisms of defense. This is more likely to happen when individuals are young children and their repertoire of *protective behavior is limited*; therefore, they resort to mechanisms of defense, such as, repression, denial, projection, reaction-formation and undoing.

Defenses distort a person's perceptions of reality—this is a cost. At the same time these defenses can be usefully protective—and this, of course, is a gain. When these ominous situations are direr and are experienced as life threatening, the child feels terrified, freezes and dissociates. In these latter situations, we identify the child as being *traumatized*.

The somatic processes of dissociation and ego mechanisms of defense are similar in many ways. Usually the person curtails their breathing during these processes. Muscles are tightened that are related to movements that might be a part of flight or fight reactions to extremely threatening situations.

As an example, if their parent is abusing them as a child, and the child's reaction is to run away, and the parent forbids this movement by physical threats, the child may well tighten the muscles in his legs. This helps him not to run and to avoid the additional trauma of being beaten. If the child is repeatedly threatened in this same manner, these muscles in the legs become chronically hypertonic. *This chronic hyper-tonicity was called armoring by Reich.*

Candace Pert (Pert 97) has played an essential research role in studying the place of the body in cognitive processes. Led by an initial interest in neuropeptides, ligands and receptor cells, Pert conceptualized that decisions about which memories become conscious and which are relegated to the unconscious is influenced at the cell receptor level throughout the body. Thus cognitive process is not confined to the central nervous system. The memories that do not become conscious are stored in the muscles. Pert's concepts of cognitive process occurring throughout the body and the storage of unconscious memories in the muscles support ISP concepts and interventions rather directly.

Armoring—which, in essence, is the process that Pert is describing, in which unconscious memories are stored in the musculature of the body—occurs in segments or hoops in the body. There are seven segments: the eyes, mouth, throat, chest, diaphragm, stomach and pelvis (the legs are seen as an extension of the pelvis).

As muscles tighten to form these constricting hoops, the flow of psychobioenergy is impeded; this is what armoring achieves. In many people, the flow of energy is so hampered that it is mostly stopped and there is no awareness of the armoring. This is parallel to how ego mechanisms of defense operate. The person is also unaware of the ego mechanisms of defense. The flow of energy is only felt when the energy level is increased dramatically by physically challenging activity and/or intense emotion.

In addition to the seven segments or hoops described above, armoring appears in other patterns, which also impede the flow of energy. For example, many of the muscles in the back may be armored in a front/

back "split". This stops energy from flowing in the back and hinders the awareness and expression of angry feelings.

Again, fully established armoring is not consciously experienced. The person is not aware of the lack of sensation engendered by this armoring, just as ego mechanisms of defense are also not consciously experienced. If the armoring or defenses were conscious, they would not do their work effectively. Then a person becomes aware that something is occurring which they did not allow themselves to become aware. This awareness is tantamount to the failure of the defenses and of the armoring because the person becomes alerted to the warded off impulses, thoughts and feelings.

ISP works to reduce the spasticity of armored muscles. As this spasticity is addressed by body interventions, the patient gains access to the "forgotten" memories. In this way, ISP promotes a healing integration of the body and of these unconscious memories and their attendant emotions and actions.

Exercise Interventions

I have introduced you to two types of somatic interventions that reduce armoring: direct touch (soft, containing and hard), and spontaneous movement. Now we turn to a third type of somatic intervention: using structured positions or exercises.

In an exercise intervention, the patient is presented with a specific position. The therapist demonstrates the form by taking the position first. Then the therapist coaches the patient to take the prescribed position. The first position we will learn is the *Sensing Position*.

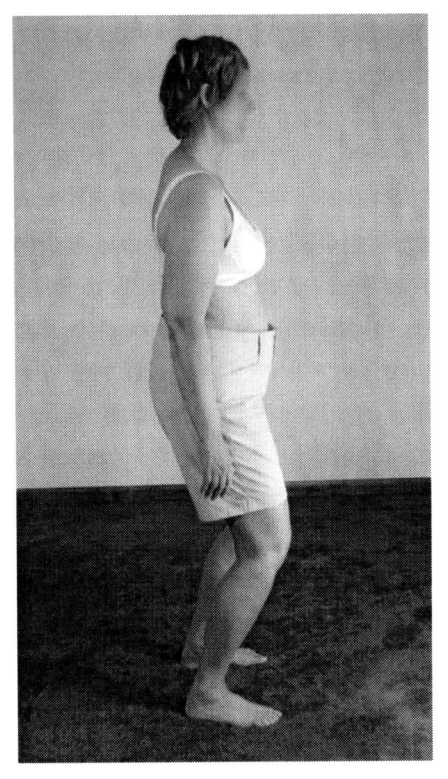

The Sensing Position

Illustration 1. The Sensing Position

The patient is asked to parallel his feet about a shoulder width apart. He bends his knees noticeably, and lets his arms and hands hang down in a relaxed manner. His head is held upright and relaxed. He rotates his pelvis backwards and under. His upper body is upright, also in a relaxed position. He breathes deeply from his nose and mouth slowly, while his mouth is held open.

This position, aided by deep breathing, maximizes the person's awareness of his inner experience and intensifies attendant emotions. The effects of this position also increase the readiness of earlier, unconscious experiences to come into consciousness because the memories are being mobilized or strengthened.

I often use this posture to initiate the body-based part of the therapy session. This position may also be used before and after a run of body experiences to bring the patient's attention to the somatic and psychological impact of the bodywork just completed. The patient can do a comparison of what he experiences between the starting Sensing Position and the finishing Sensing Position to capture the impact of the work he has done.

The next two postures are paired *Stress Positions*. The first of the pair is called the Backward Bow. The second is called the Forward Arch.

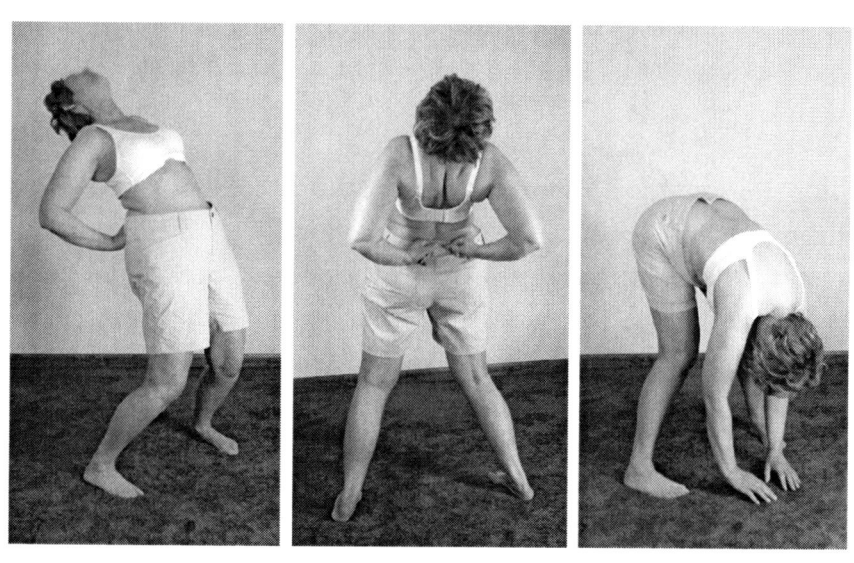

The Backward Bow and the Forward Arch

Illustration 2. The Backward Bow and the Forward Arch

Here the patient is asked to move his feet so they are shoulder width apart, then to slant his heels out. He is told to make two fists and place them on his back, waist-high. The fists are placed vertically and he pushes them into his back. In this way he pushes the middle of his body forward. He leans his head back, which continues arching the middle of his body forward. He is asked to open his mouth and breathe through his nose and mouth, breathing deeply and slowly. He is asked to open his chest by pushing his elbows together. From the side, his body looks like a bow that is curved by pulling on an imagined string.

When the patient tires in this position, he moves directly into the Forward Arch. The person is told to remove his fists from his back. He extends his fingers and moves his hands and arms in an upward arc and then forward. Then his fingertips touch the floor lightly in front of his feet. He lets his head go forward so that it is relaxed in an upside down, vertical position. Again, he opens his mouth and breathes deeply and slowly through his mouth and nose. His heels remain slanted out.

This stress position is intense. It often stirs up feelings and deepens them much more than the Sensing Position does. Forgotten and repressed thoughts are thrust into consciousness. Sometimes, from this position, the patient is thrust into action, which eventuates in a reduction of the increased energy charge when the action is completed. What emerges in the patient during this stress position may initiate and stimulate the rest of the body session, where touch work and spontaneous movement may occur.

Stress positions can be painful, especially if the person is heavily armored. He is told to lean into his limits, not to try to abruptly break through them. If he appears to take flight from this work, he is encouraged to stay longer or he is told to do the positions again. Eventually, in the therapy, the muscles of his arms, legs and trunk relax, and his body starts to vibrate. The vibration indicates that the person's energy flows more fully and freely than before these exercises were done. Doing the stress positions decrease the person's armoring by consecutively stretching and compressing the muscles of the body that contain unconscious emotions and early experiences. This sequential stretching and compression of muscles fosters de-armoring and *the healing of the person.*

The next exercises, the side-to-side movement and stress exercise are even more intensely grounding than the backward bow and forward arch. So if a patient lacks grounding, a therapist can sequence the side-to-side stress positions after the patient gets major benefits, from the backward bow and forward arch.

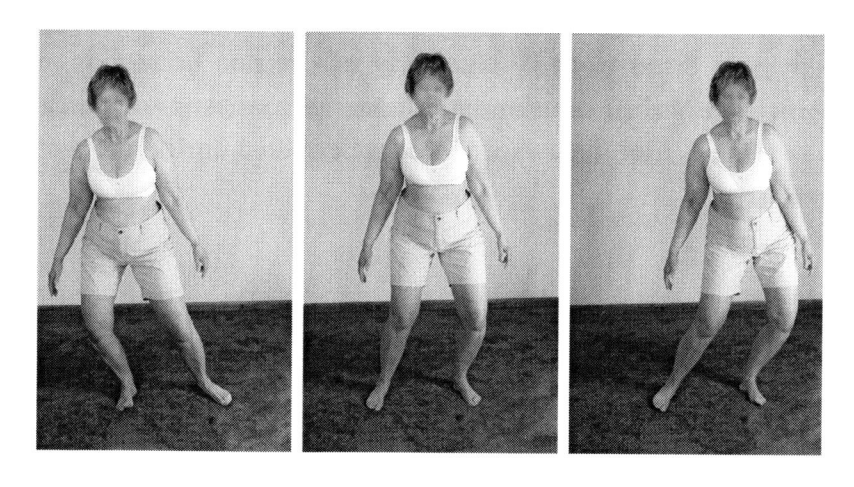

The Side-to-Side Movement and Stress Position

<u>Illustration 3. The Side-to-Side Movement and Stress Position</u>

The patient is asked to stand with his feet parallel, a little more than a foot apart. He is asked to let his knees bend deeply. Then he moves his knees horizontally to the floor in an arc from one side to the other. His legs move so that at the extremes he is on the sides of his two feet. One foot is on the outside edge, while the other foot is on the inside edge. This movement is called the Side-to-Side movement.

After the patient's feet loosen up, he is asked to stop the movement at one extreme and hold it until he is fatigued; this is the side-to side stress position. The patient shakes his two legs out to relax them. Then he is asked to go back to the position with his feet parallel. He bends his knees again. Once more he moves his knees in an arc that is horizontal to the floor. He is asked to move to the other side and to hold this position. The stress position ends when his feet and legs tire. This ends the Side-to-Side Stress Position.

This stress position is more intensely grounding than the Backward Bow and the Forward Arch. Stress work is initiated early in the therapy, because grounding is required to do the intense work of therapy. Stress work is done early in a session because it may spontaneously elicit experiences that are not conscious but are close to awareness. And these experiences are explored during the rest of the session.

CHAPTER 2

ISP's Core Treatment Processes

Most sessions start with the patient reporting what has happened to him since his last session. The therapist mostly listens carefully and occasionally responds empathically. The therapist notices what the patient says and how he says it. She is noticing the cues in his narrative—for example, is the patient speaking with emotion? Or is he coming mostly from his head? The therapist finds clues as to where in the patient's body she might intervene with touch, if the session comes to this. Does the patient talk in an intensely emotional way about his work in the last session, i.e., does he need to continue working on those experiences today? The useful clues for the therapist may be a few among a very large variety of patient behavior. It is important for the therapist to listen carefully and to notice what clues are important to her. This is primarily an intuitive process.

As we are affected by our culture, we often push ourselves to act the way *we should or want to be*. Either type of action is very different from *allowing*. Allowing is the gateway process into the *Self*.

(The action of allowing can be developed and supported by practicing activities such as meditation. With some patients who have difficulty "allowing," I have trained them to meditate and to do it outside of the psychotherapy sessions.)

Allowing experiences to occur is important because it fosters self-awareness. Practicing allowing in successive experiences promotes the development of this skill. The patient is told to notice their experience, which elicits a passive stance, and supports allowing. Being more active—self-consciously trying or pushing oneself to become, is a part of the more executive aspect of the personality, the *Ego*. By contrast, we spend much time in the first stage of ISP therapy settling into and exploring the *Self*. Later, during the second stage of ISP therapy, we explore the ego's style, standards and ideals. Then we focus on aiding the integration of the Ego and Self so that they function collaboratively.

This important ISP process, inner experiencing, is often entered into at the early part of a session. Inner experience is a major highway along which significant healing and human expansion occurs. Specifically, the content of this process is first determined by the patient's initial report. If the patient is still triggered by the last session's incomplete work, then this will be the content of their process. If they had a dream or a partially recovered early memory, then this is the focus of their process.

If the patient is not triggered in the early part of the session, then he is asked to do stress work while breathing deeply. We are seeking experiences that have an important *feeling* component. Doing stress work often facilitates unconscious experiences to emerge that are close to consciousness. At the same time the stress work increases the patient's grounding, which enables him to go into emotionally charged experiences. This yields the content of the initial process.

If stress work does not elicit an intense experience or memory from the patient, the therapist may choose to do deep tissue massage work. Often, this brings into awareness the patient's unconscious and strong feelings about an earlier childhood experience. Doing deep tissue touch work elicits these memories quickly by evoking regression in the patient. This becomes the content for the patient's process. Since a crucial part of ISP is to aid patients in finishing their early traumatic experiences, deep touch is an important ISP intervention.

The Awareness Cycle[*]—Once the patient launches into an emotional inner experience, the Awareness Cycle helps to structure the processing of their experience. This cycle has five steps: Self-Awareness, Self-Acknowledgment, Self-Acceptance, ([Congruent] Action) and Self-Appreciation. Let's explore the cycle by understanding the individual steps more fully.

1. Self-Awareness—Once the content is identified, the Awareness Cycle starts with the patient becoming aware that he is having an experience. The experience may include strong feelings, thoughts, memories and action tendencies. I ask the patient *to just notice* the experience (that is to allow the experience to happen without consciously trying to change it). Often, the patient does not fully recognize that they are having a significant experience. So I ask him to just notice the thoughts, feelings, memories and actions tendencies that emerge. Cultivating the capacity to just allow one's experience to happen is crucial for the person to develop deeper levels of

---

[*] I am indebted to the work of John Weir (Mix 2006) who developed an Awareness Model for his workshop titled Self-Differentiation. The model I present here is <u>derived</u> from Weir's concepts. Twice, I staffed this workshop with him and his wife, Joyce.

awareness of experiences. I support patients in just allowing themselves to experience. I readily accept whatever emerges for the patient. I am supporting the spontaneity of the patient. It takes practice over a series of sessions for the person to allow himself to go deeply into his experiences.

2. Self-Acknowledgement—Here the focus is on the person taking fuller ownership of what he is experiencing at a deeper level. The spontaneity of the person's experience affirms that he is contacting a deeper part of himself. I respond empathically to the specifics of his experience and affirm that it reflects a deeper part of the person, his self. The experience is more useful and powerful if the person acknowledges its importance in front of me, to himself, and by saying it out loud.

3. Self-Acceptance—Accepting that whatever he is experiencing at this deeper level is fully legitimate for him. So he supports his experience, as I do.

4. (Congruent Action)—Once the first three steps of the awareness cycle occur, the probability is high that the person will take action that is consistent with what has emerged during these previous steps. The person's action often occurs spontaneously and the feeling of "fit" becomes very obvious to him. If the person does not move on to this action step, I may stimulate him with a question, such as, "knowing this about yourself now, what do you do or what are you likely to do"? Taking action is very important for the person because it is a culmination within the cycle of awareness. Developmental change is not merely a matter of insight—mere insight is not enough to transform a person's life so that they are living with greater integrity with respect to their deeper self. Integrity is an expression of congruence in the sense that one's behavior matches one's inner experience. Living in the world effectively requires one to act in a genuine way, acting from his deeper self.

5. Self-Appreciation—Here the person values himself for moving into and through the Awareness Cycle. This work is not easy. Initially, the person may feel quite anxious because he does not know where his experience will take him until the experience is finished. Yet, the commitment to proceed is required before he knows fully what his journey will be. The size of the risk is also unknown until the person takes it. Importantly, the person gradually learns that he has the resources to carry him through, and the courage to proceed, even though he may feel a high level of anxiety. Self-appreciation is not always done after each Awareness Cycle. If the person goes through a number of cycles in a session, then the self-appreciation may occur at the wrap-up of the session.

Paradoxical Change

Going through an awareness cycles eventuates in the patient being increasingly aware of himself. As this self-awareness deepens, the person may move into *paradoxical change*. I refer to this process as paradoxical change because, by living more fully into his experience of self with clarity, the person opens himself up to moving into and through the experience, and, ultimately to changing. This is a spontaneous process.

As a person repeatedly goes through the Awareness Cycle, his levels of self-trust and *courage* increase gradually. Eventually, the person feels less anxious because he knows increasingly that he has what it takes to proceed fully and successfully. In this way, patients gradually increase their *courage* to proceed during the course of their psychotherapy. At the same time, this repeated cycling leads to a progression of going down deeper into the Self.

Jerry Perlmutter, PhD

An Introduction to the Exploration of the Soul and Spirit

Journeying down into the deep Self eventually leads to encountering the person's Soul. I see the Soul as the deepest core of the Self. Physically or somatically, this is a movement down into the deep belly and pelvis. Eastern philosophy and religion names this area, the *Hara*. The Soul is the pattern of deep beliefs, awareness's and knowledge in the core Self. Soulful contact also expands our feeling of connection to human beings, to other living creatures and also to the earth. We also may feel connected to the "divine". When we are soulful, we move more *gracefully* through the world.

The *energy* connected to the Soul's pattern is called the *Spirit*. As we descend into our soul, we gain access to much greater streams of our energy and to a much fuller awareness and connection to our deeper resources. This quest leads to a sense of Self, which liberates the energy to pursue this inner depth. *This often makes the arduous journey worthwhile!*

Not every patient chooses to go this far in exploring his or her soul and spirit. As therapists, we learn to accept that this is an important right of patients. Patients experience their souls differently from each other, and we must accept this too. There is no one established pattern of soul. This unique journey towards greater courage is a cornerstone of our work with people. As ISP therapists, we provide the support that comes from the gradual and paced expansion of courage that prepares the person to live a life of greater creativity and self-commitment.

In summary, this chapter has focused on *the Awareness Cycle, a core process of ISP*. This cycle is crucial to the treatment done by ISP practitioners. The process of this cycle supports the deepening of inner experiences, and this promotes a frequently used change process in ISP, paradoxical change. Paradoxical change happens when a person is *very deeply aware* of their inner experience, and then they spontaneously change. Another way of describing paradoxical change is that a person finishes with a feeling by going fully into the feeling experience and through it to another place. This is not planned change (which is ego directed); it is "spontaneous change", and transformative. The paradox of change will be explored more, further on in this book. The Awareness Cycle and the paradox of change merit this full chapter devoted to them because they comprise a primary core of ISP.

CHAPTER 3

ISP and the Treatment of Character

Traumas Shape Character

Integrative Somatic Psychotherapy has been developed to treat and change character. Character refers to the basic style of the individual, i.e., the usual way a person reacts and acts across the broad scope of their life. Character encompasses enduring perceptions and assumptions about self, others and the perceived nature of the relationships between self and others. The character of the person reflects a narrowing of their repertoire of actions and reactions, given their much broader potential resources. Character accounts for the predictability of an individual's behavior.

People get rigidly committed to a narrower range of behavior because it worked so successfully in earlier, difficult and frustrating circumstances. These circumstances occur early in life when the organism is young, undeveloped and limited in terms of potential response possibilities; or later in life by *catastrophic* events that few, if any, can master or respond to adequately. Extremely difficult and frustrating circumstances for the young, and catastrophes for adults (e.g., extreme storms, starvation, confinement in a concentration camp), are both referred to as *trauma*[*]. Traumas and our reactions to them play a major role in shaping character. ISP has been developed in part to help individuals to heal from trauma so that they expand the richness of their lives.

Trauma shapes character based upon when the trauma occurred during the development of the person and the type of trauma experienced. Traumas that occur early in infancy limit the individual's capacity to form relationships with others, to initiate integrated behavior and to be self-accepting.

Sexual trauma experienced during the early years has a numbing effect on feelings, a freezing effect on action and a disorienting effect on awareness of self in the world. This numbness accompanies the experience of terror, which is an intense fear of dying. The child feels that he or she is faced with death by being exposed to sexual experiences that they are much too immature to understand and to cope with psychologically and physically. Often these experiences are accompanied by aggression from the perpetrator who pressures the child into submitting to being used sexually. Very often perpetrators severely threaten the child to keep the child from revealing the adult's sexual assaults to other adults. This is an initial description of the PTSD process that entails child sexual assault.

I had a patient who had her initial sexual assault by her father when she was two years old. Imagine the confusion and the excruciating physical pain she experienced being sexually penetrated at that age. In addition to the ongoing trauma of the assaults themselves,

---

[*] These trauma occur because the individual is intensely abused to the point of being annihilated. The accompanying feeling is terror. Trauma also occurs when the person witnesses a loved one being abused also to the extreme of being annihilated. Here the person feels horror.

throughout her childhood this patient also had to mute her responses to keep her father's assaults a secret, as he continually threatened to kill her if she disclosed the assaults to anyone.

The Psychoanalytic Perspective of Character Formation

Reichian and neo-Reichian approaches to body psychotherapy are rooted in psychoanalytic theory. This theory is based on a view of personality development that is primarily shaped during the first six years of life. Character is formed by repeated deprivations that occur during specific *stages* of infancy and childhood that Freud referred to as psychosexual. These earlier stages are named oral, anal and phallic. (Actually, Reichian therapy and the Reichian based therapies that followed have introduced an earlier phase of development that they name the *visual stage.*) The manner in which these stages are traversed is paramount in influencing the nature of the personality and, more specifically, the character of the individual. Freud used the term psychosexual because he focused on the sexual capacity and the sexual identity of the adult in appraising the healthiness of the person.

Character is shaped by trauma and repeated deprivation, mostly by parenting figures that results in stage-specific character traits. The responses of the person to the trauma tend to be instituted powerfully in them because they are perceived as having insured the survival of the victim. And these responses tend to be used broadly in other situations throughout one's life whether they are effective or not, even though the person may have developed new possible responses based on their maturation.

Many people seek psychotherapy when their character is so limiting that they can neither successfully adapt to their world nor live a life that is sufficiently satisfying and meaningful to them. Changing character is more difficult than treating psychopathological symptoms. These strenuous efforts are worthwhile because important basic changes are made in the personality that promotes *widespread healing and development.*

The term personality is used here as a more encompassing term denoting the psychological life of the individual. Character is a part of the personality. In traditional Reichian body psychotherapy, it is important to accurately diagnose the character of the patient because treatment proceeds differently based on this distinction. Symptoms are quite different in their qualities based on the character in which they occur. Depression is different in an oral character (emotional emptiness from a lack of sufficient nurturing in infancy) versus in a schizoid (self-loathing, internalized from a parent who unconsciously hated them). Treatment is quite different in these two instances based on their divergent etiologies.

The precedent for the use of character in body psychotherapy comes from Wilhelm Reich (Reich 1949). Reich described the dynamics, etiology and body structure of various character types. The major character structures that prevail are the schizoid, oral, masochist and the phallic (which includes the phallic hysteric and the phallic narcissist).

The etiologies of character types are based upon fixations (or getting stuck) at the successive psychosexual stages elaborated in Freud's psychoanalytic theory. Reich's primary goal of treatment was to help his patients to develop into the genital character, which was conceived of in terms of being capable of performing sexual intercourse in a manner that is highly satisfying sexually and emotionally.

Current schools of body psychotherapy use Reich's formulations as a foundation for their approaches. Because they modify Reich's theories and interventions, they are often referred to as "neo-Reichian".

Examples of neo-Reichian schools of body psychotherapy include Bioenergetics (Lowen 1958), Core Energetics (Pierrakos 1990), and Organismic Psychotherapy (Brown undated) and, of course, Integrative Somatic Psychotherapy.

Using Character to Further Structure ISP Treatment

ISP is primarily focused on developing the awareness of the core process that fosters the healing and the development of the individual. The core processes are usually elicited by stress work that evokes intense inner experiences. In time, using this core process usually leads the patient to spontaneously deal with much of the content (like character) that is necessary to achieve deep healing. The therapist supports this effort and facilitates the patient to intensify and expand their experiences and their actions.

Much of the character work occurs spontaneously in reaction to somatic interventions, i.e., stress work, touch work (deep and catalytic, containing, and soft and nurturing) and spontaneous movement. Dream work also supports character exploration because dreams are totally structured by the dreamer, and therefore, can be worked at very deep and revealing levels.

As more experiences emerge in the therapy that are a part of a "character cluster," the patient recognizes, expands and deepens this structure with the psychotherapist's help. The therapist supports the patient to explore deeply each experience in a cluster of experiences. Then the therapist helps the patient to realize the interconnectedness of these character-related experiences, for example, they have the same or similar themes or they are related to the same or similarly intense early memories. These experiences are also undergirded by similar sets of assumptions.

This organization of character experiences is a "gathering together" process. This type of process is called *induction*. ISP uses induction much more than it's polarity, *deduction*. Deduction identifies connections between external behavior and implicit and often unknown (unconscious) underlying, inner processes. These connections are spelled out in the theory base of a psychotherapy approach. It takes training in the psychotherapy approach to know and be able recognize these connections as they occur in a session, i.e., it is the psychotherapist who recognizes these underlying processes, and usually interprets the underlying events that are occurring in the patient. Therefore, deduction has the therapist shaping the patient's view of his inner experience according to his theory of psychotherapy. ISP, by contrast, keeps this ownership with the patient as much as possible. I mean that we support the patient's playing the major role in recognizing the meaning of their experience. And their work is based on the commonalities that the patient identifies among their experiences (once again, this is using induction).

But patients get stuck. And that is when ISP therapists get more active in helping patients to define the meaning of their inner experiences. In this type of situation, I prefer to help by using somatic interventions that often elicit deeper experiences, which puts the patient in a better position to recognize the meaning of their experience.

As the psychotherapy proceeds, patients are increasingly capable of experiencing and identifying their inner life. And part of the therapy, the patient pays a cognitive and creative role in defining these important aspects of the Self: inner experience and inner structure. After the therapy is terminated, patients ease into continuing this self-discovery and inner structuring work by themselves. This leads them to living deeply and to continuing to alter themselves by working with new outer and inner experiences.

As a way of particularizing the character theory to fit the unique qualities of each patient, ISP is heavily focused on the *processes* of psychotherapeutic change and healing. While character theory has a lot of content to it, it is entered into when the patient *spontaneously* arrives at character clusters, or character-related experiences and groupings of character experiences.

Healing Trauma to Reduce Character Strictures

Character clusters are very often associated with a specific part of the body. For example, missing sufficient mothering, feeling unworthy of love, low self-esteem and rounded shoulders and a collapsed chest co-occur in a depressive/oral character. This association aids the therapist in developing body-based interventions that help the patient to further their character exploration. For example, doing deep tissue work to the patient's shoulder muscles and the intercostal muscles between the ribs are likely to trigger regression and to make the depressive issues starkly conscious to the patient.

This *regression* provides the opportunity for the patient to re-experience their trauma. This re-experiencing aids the completing of the earlier trauma and the reduction/elimination of character limitations. Specifically, the patient has not fully enough *known what happened to him* when he was being traumatized, *nor fully felt and expressed the feelings* he had then; and did not fully *act on what he needed to do then*. Again, in order to effect this completion, the patient must regress and re-experience and redo the trauma much more fully in these three dimensions italicized in the previous sentence.

If patients remember traumatic experiences without completing them, they usually feel depressed and more hopeless. In trauma work, we build *on a natural occurring process of remembering incomplete experiences again and again (hopefully) until they are completed.*

Touch work on the parts of the body associated with the trauma helps the patient to regress and to experience the trauma more deeply and completely. The chronically tense (armored) muscles that numb from the trauma experiences are softened and the defenses are hereby reduced. We refer to this whole process as: *Regressing, Re-experiencing, Redoing and Completing*.

The way that ISP proceeds, which integrates many of the facets of self-exploration (the Awareness Cycle) and the completion of trauma is crucial to this work. As an illustration, lets go back to the presentation of Steve (on page 15).

Let's review the sequence of his work so that we can proceed. Steve brings himself to experience his intense anger at his father for leaving him and his mother when he was a year old. He goes deeper and deeper into his anger and expresses his anger more fully by invoking his father facing him on the mattress on the wall opposite to him. He yells at and punches and kicks his father over a series of sessions. His expression of his anger deepens. Then suddenly Steve is flooded with feelings of sadness from his father abandoning him. He mourns his father's leaving.

This sudden shift in Steve's feelings from anger to sadness is where Steve experiences the *paradox of change*. His shift is spontaneous and does not require the therapist or Steve to identify when he has finished with his anger. This spontaneous shift leads to change that is *transformational*. He has finished dealing with his anger! This paradoxical change facilitates the deepest experiencing of his angry action and his sad feelings so that he completes this trauma and can move on.

While Steve cannot forgive his father because he had no more contact with him, he recognizes that he did not know the relationship that his mother and father had. He is able to move on knowing that his mother took the responsibility of raising him: this deepens his respect and love for his mother. In the cases presented in the remainder of this book, you will repeatedly read about persons who have had this transformational shift facilitated by the paradox of change as they work their childhood trauma.

Some Further Clarity about the Use of Character in ISP

When I was first trained as a body psychotherapist, I was exposed to and used Reich's, Lowen's, and early Brown's approaches. I searched the patient's body structure and their regression experiences to identify the character of my patient. I used the identified character to help the patient move on to new facets of their character's exploration. The identified character helped me to move the patient to focus on ensuing experiences that filled out the dynamics of the character. I used character theory more deductively in my early days of practice, versus my later use of a much more inductive approach.

Some Cautions Before We Proceed

Character Nomenclature

I have doubts about the use of the psychoanalytic names given to the characters: schizoid, masochistic, phallic narcissist and the phallic hysteric (and not with the oral). To me, these names imply that a great deal of psychopathology is being assigned to persons who have been identified with these character names. This is not my intention when I diagnose the character of a person. I am identifying that all individuals with the same character share a pattern of personality traits and body structures. The degree of psychopathology varies widely among persons given the same character name. For example, persons who are labeled schizoid will range from individuals that have very creative and spiritual personalities to those who have schizophrenia with active delusions and the severe splitting off of thoughts from feelings.

I see two choices: change the names to more descriptive names, or use the traditional names, but avoid sharing these names with patients, lest they believe that they are being judged as "very sick". I prefer the latter course because I can be more consistent with earlier Freudian psychoanalytic practitioners, with Reichian, and some neo-Reichian body psychotherapists*. I have used the patient's own character-related terminology to develop and use a character name as I work with a patient. For example, in the past, a patient and I referred to him as an *overly controlled* person in his relationship with his mother. As a result, he overly controls himself now. And he also frequently overly controls others. This approach was used for a masochistic character.

The Complexity of Character Types

The vast majority of people have aspects of more than one character. I have rarely worked with anyone that fit into only one category of character. Thus, one usually works in ISP with a few character types during the course of psychotherapy. I work first on the character that is most available to the patient, which makes the work with this character easier for the patient. This also provides the patient with assurance that they are capable of doing character work. Most persons are capable of doing this work if they can proceed gradually, at a pace that is not overwhelming.

---

* I owe a professional debt to these practitioners because my work has built upon theirs. I refer specifically to Alexander Lowen and Malcolm Brown. Other clinicians, such as Stephen M. Johnson and Ron Kurtz have created new character labels for their approaches.

Jerry Perlmutter, PhD

Healing Character by Externalizing Introjects

A necessary ingredient of character-based body psychotherapy is the separation of the patient from their psychologically internalized parent(s), or introjects. These introjects have a widespread impact on a patient's life; this is especially so because the introject functions unconsciously, and therefore is often unchecked or reality tested. The introject is an ever present force in the person that keeps them powerfully tied to their past. Ongoing messages from our introjects influence our deepest set of assumptions about life, i.e., our self, others and the perceived nature of the relationships between our self and others.

Another Caution Before We Deal with Character Based Psychotherapy

Please do not expect that reading about character treatment alone will teach you to do Integrative Somatic Psychotherapy. If you have been trained to do body psychotherapy, you may incorporate into your work some of the processes described here. You may use some of the specific interventions described here, too. However, it is imperative that you are personally and professionally prepared to deal with intense emotional experiences of your patients as you adopt some of the approach described here. Having an effective, personal body psychotherapy helps you prepare to do this, especially if your therapy is searching and depthful. If you work with individuals in this way that elicits intense emotional states, and you are not able to deal therapeutically with what arises, you are functioning *unethically*, to my reckoning.

Why Use Character Types in this Book?

Character types identify ISP's historical foundation with Reich. Character structure and its therapeutic approach are used in this book to show how the therapist can sequence interventions in body psychotherapy. (This is how I initially learned to sequence interventions in my early therapy sessions.) *Be aware that the patients presented in this book have been worked with using ISP, i.e. inductively, using paradoxical change, and spontaneous change, etc.* These patients have been selected for two reasons: they come close to having one character, and they are more recent patients of mine.

The Structure of the Character Treatment Sections that Follow

Each chapter that follows will start with an outline of the character being presented. The outline will start with the *etiology* or the origins of the character. Then the *body structure and the personality of* the character are summarized. Last, the treatment of a patient with the designated character is presented.

Specific touches and exercises are presented for each character. These are only examples that are used to concretize the approach of Integrative Somatic Psychotherapy. There are many more interventions than the ones presented in this book. The full spectrum of interventions is taught in training programs in body psychotherapy, especially if the treatment approach is neo-Reichian.

A Practicality

Doing sessions that become more intense with time in therapy has led me to do sessions lasting seventy-five minutes. Patients need time to bring themselves psychologically into the session milieu. Then they need sufficient time to do their work. Patients then prepare themselves to return to their everyday world. The usual fifty-minute session is not sufficient to do all of these tasks.

CHAPTER 4

Treating the Oral Character

Etiology

As an infant (first year of life), their parents did not meet their basic needs—this is a failure of nurturing. Possibly, during the first year of life, the child was separated from the mother—or the mother was quite sick or depressed or she had to leave the home. Maybe the child got sick and had a very great need for nurturing that the mother couldn't meet. Sometimes parent(s) are psychologically inadequate or insufficient caregivers. These are all possible circumstances that lead to this character's continuing passive, oral hunger. He feels empty inside. He believes that he is entitled to being satisfied by others. Moreover, he does not give much back to others. An early parenting failure leads him to mistrust others. In addition, these circumstances may lead to an extended immaturity into childhood and adulthood that is based upon his fantasies of dependent gratification.

The child may develop a facade of independence that can extend into adulthood. This has been labeled the *compensated oral.*

The continued real lack of gratification of strong dependency needs leads to deep feelings of hopelessness in the oral character.

What may ensue is a cycle of depression based on the underlying feeling of hopelessness of getting real oral gratification, followed by elation based on fantasies and hopes of dependent gratification. This is the basis of the bi-polar personality.

This character type may develop eating or alcohol addictions related to their feelings of emptiness.

Somatic Aspects of the Oral

Their lack of satisfaction leads to a lack of energy. The oral does not build-up an energy charge—they are under-contained, their energy dribbles away.

Their focus is on their head. The head is separated from the body by a ring of armoring at the base of the skull. The muscles at the base of the skull are chronically tight, as are their jaw muscles—this is called the oral ring where the pain from the lack of "oral feeding" is numbed by armoring

As an adult, the oral person talks a lot and may overeat. He frequently figures things out in his head. When he walks he leads with his head. All these actions express the prominence of their head in the oral's life.

The oral's chest is soft and deflated. Their stomach is soft, as well. Their back is weak. The long muscles of the back become rigid to protect against the collapse of their back. The openness in the front of the body reflects the person's high potential for being empathic and spiritual.

The oral's legs are both weak and are tight. The knees are also locked to counter their strong tendency to collapse. Their arches are collapsed. Their lack of grounding is a focal issue.

Treatment of the Oral

This type of patient often seeks psychotherapy because they feel depressed and hopeless.

The ISP therapist is emotionally available to their patient for bonding. Perlmutter (2010, pp. 11 & 12) writes:

> Mahler (69, 72 et al 75) describes a sequence of child development stages that focus on the evolution of the ego. The scheme was derived from observing children. The child moves from autism, then a symbiotic relationship with her mother, to separation and individuation.
>
> We use Mahler's scheme to directly guide our psychotherapeutic behavior with patients. The patient's stage of ego development is assessed. Then the "good enough" parent's behavior that fosters the child to move on to the next ego stage of development is adopted by the therapist...
>
> This [oral] patient suffers from a lack of a symbiotic connection to her mother (usually occurs between two and six months of age)…As her psychotherapist I give her much soft touch. I am very empathic

when she expresses feelings. I clearly acknowledge her needs and support her right to have and express these. I use my intuition to identify needs that she is not expressing directly. These are all behaviors that support the patient in having a symbiotic connection to me.

The patient becomes capable of closer relationships as his treatment proceeds. Towards the end of sessions, before having the patient do grounding positions, the therapist uses soft, nurturing touch, and containing touch (to counter the patient's tendency to be under-contained). Containing touch is a soft touch to large amounts of the patient's body surface. An example is giving soft touch to the patient's chest using the therapist's chest to make contact.

Increasing grounding is a crucial aspect of the therapy of an oral patient. Starting therapy with grounding work increases the patient's capability of doing the deep work required to heal. Doing the sensing position is a beginning opportunity to work on grounding in a low-key way.

Using the side-to-side stress position fosters a deeper level of groundedness than the sensing position and the backward bow and forward arch. These positions have a natural sequence that depends on the gradual loosening of leg and pelvic muscles by developmentally moving from less to more demanding activities.

The side-to-side stress position very powerfully increases patients' grounding. By practicing the sequence of stress positions until they are mastered, the stamina of the patient is greatly increased and his tendency to collapse is reduced

The Injustice of the Lack of Nurturance

I resonate with patients' feelings of injustice, whether it is a parent's fault or due to circumstances beyond the control of humans. No child asks to come into the world. And if the child is harmed as an infant, it is an injustice no matter how it occurred, whether his mother was killed by a storm or any other natural catastrophe that interfered with the infant's care. Therefore, I find it easy and natural to empathize with oral patient's feelings of being needy.

Working Out the Feelings of Past Anger and Pain

It is necessary for the patient to identify who or what inflicted the pain or victimized him. Very likely this is an introject. It could be a parent or both parents, each taken separately. It could be god or lady luck. We shouldn't guess whom. The patient will tell himself and us as he begins this work, when he gets into his feelings.

Sequencing Anger and Pain Work

It is not unusual for patients to quickly move from expressing their anger to expressing their pain before they are finished expressing their anger. The effect of doing this is to truncate the anger work, and thereby to limit healing. It is important for the therapist to monitor this process and to support the patient in expressing his anger until it is mostly diminished. Some people have a tendency to avoid expressing intense anger. Working on their anger until it is more fully expressed, helps the patient to break through this limitation. In our society, women are more likely to be socialized in a way that makes it easier for them express sadness when they feel anger. Expressing anger fully in therapy helps to counter the dysfunctional and limiting female sex role to which many women have been socialized.

Healing Body, Self and Soul

The Use of Specific Body Interventions

Using the guideline of working head down towards the tail, I start work at the head/neck. The armoring of the oral ring fosters the isolation of the head. To integrate the patient's head with her body, it is important to use deep touch to the muscles at the base of the skull and at the jaw joints. It is often useful to then proceed directly to doing hard touch to the long muscles of the back (this certainly fits for the patient presented at the end of this chapter. The next touch is one that can be used in this sequencing for the oral.

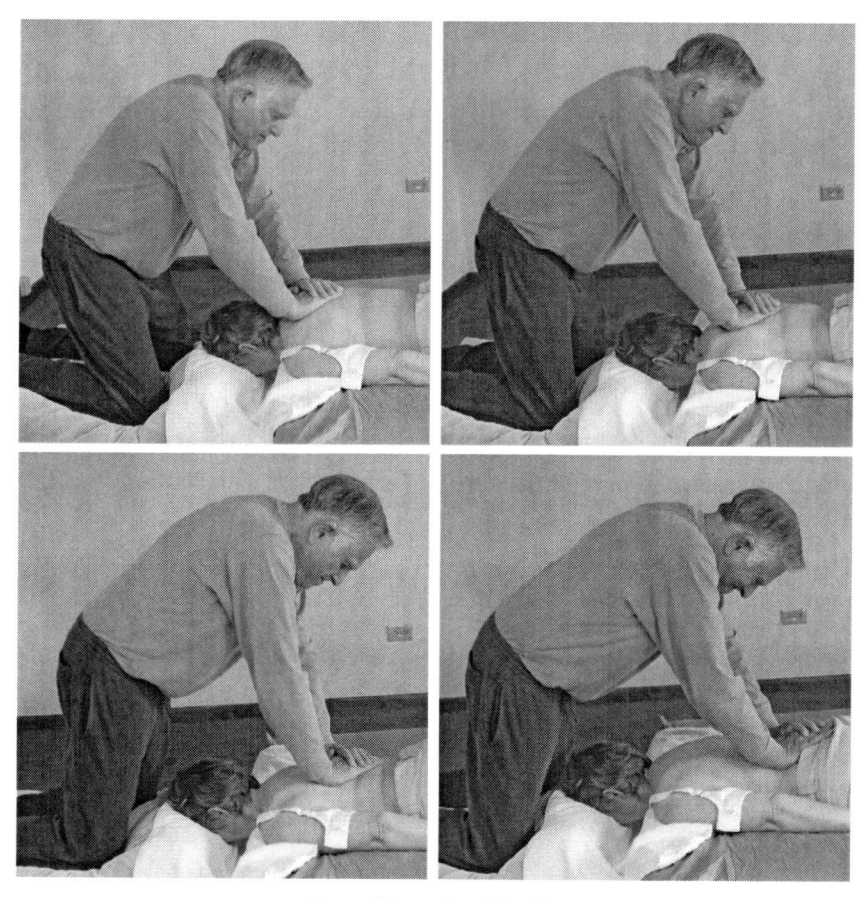

Leveling the Back

Illustration 4. Leveling the Back

The patient is asked to lie on his stomach in the prone position. The therapist moves onto his knees at the head of his patient. He puts lotion on the palms of his hands. He breathes in unison with his patient. He crosses his fingers and uses his palms to move starting from just below her shoulders down to the waist along the long muscles of his patient's back. His crossed fingers help the therapist to not touch the patient's spine as he does this touch. He comes up on his knees and leans over his hands to put pressure on her muscles as she starts exhaling. He does this touch about three times. Using the stroke on the patient's exhale elongates her exhale and deepens her breathing. This touch by itself can be very therapeutic by loosening the armoring of the patient's back, and deepening her breathing, which thereby increases her vital capacity. The patient's energy and capacity to act is also increased. Grounding supports her taking action as well.

These deep tissue touches are complex and difficult to do effectively. In a training group, the trainer first models these touches. Then groups of three trainees are employed to teach these interventions in practice sessions. The trainee that is touched and the third member, the onlooker, both provide feedback on how well the touch was done and what was the impact of the touch on the patient/trainee. I suggest that readers, who are interested in using these touches in their practices, seek out relevant training experiences.

At this point the therapist may alternate touches, by doing a soft, containing touch, such as Heart to Heart.

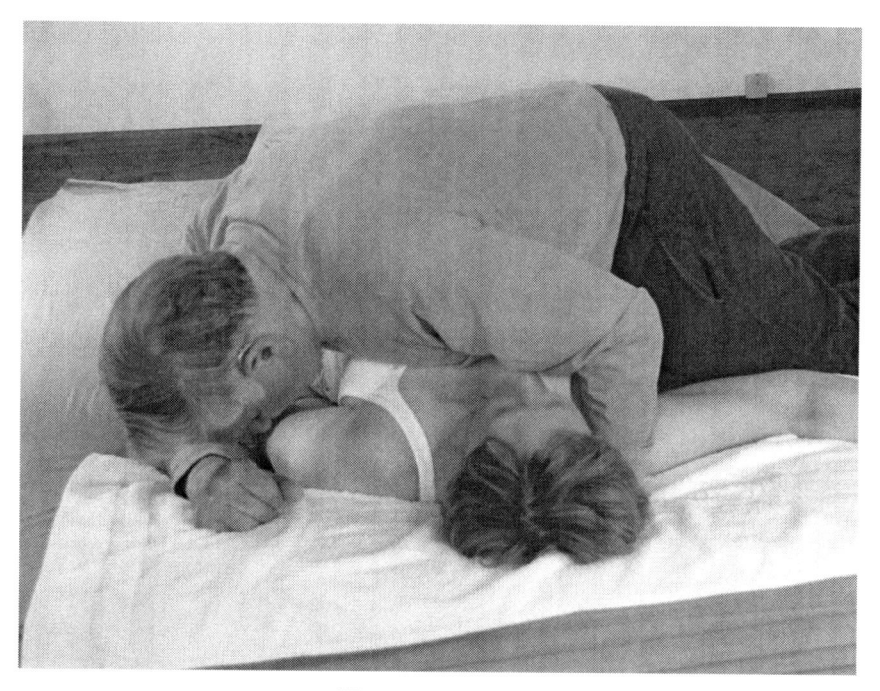

Heart to Heart

Illustration 5. Heart to Heart

This touch is a soft touch to both parts of the body that were previously given deep touch. The patient lies down in a supine position on a mattress. The therapist kneels down on his side facing his patient. He puts his hand under his patient's neck in a cradling touch. He comes over his patient touching his chest to her chest while he leans on his right forearm and knees so that he can control how much weight he gives to his patient's chest. He mirrors his patient's breathing. This is an intense soft and containing touch. This touch supports the experience of softer feelings, such as love or sadness.

If the patient feels softer feelings, the therapist can maintain contact with her for a while. Then the therapist supports the patient going deeper into her soft feelings by empathizing with her. He verbally mirrors her feelings using expressions that are verbalized more intensely than the expressions of the patient. This is a healing touch in that it is a caring touch. The therapist's use of a containing touch of the patient helps her to be more contained and this is a healing impact, too.

A patient will likely respond with loving feelings from a soft touch. Whatever feelings are actually elicited, the therapist supports their fuller expression. The therapist does not prescribe feelings and readily accepts being surprised by patients.

Giving soft after deep touches is an attempt to elicit softer feelings once angry feelings are fully expressed and acted upon. The intent is to proceed in a way that develops feeling experience and expression in a balanced and fuller manner.

The therapist may then move to his patient's softer belly. He can use containing touch again by making soft contact with his patient's belly using his belly as she lies down in a supine position. He supports and deepens all feeling expressions that emerge from this touch, as he does in the touches above.

The next touch deals with the armoring on the patient's legs. The patient again lies down on the mattress in a supine position. The therapist kneels on his knees. He asks his patient to raise her legs with her knees bent. The therapist grabs both of her feet by their arches. He tells the patient to alternatively try to straighten each leg while he resists her effort, using his body weight to hamper her. This intervention helps to strengthen her legs and to increase her grounding.

Again, it is important to emphasize that we are only detailing a fraction of the touches used during the course of a therapy. Other touches will be presented in the treatment of the other characters in the ensuing chapters.

Self-Nurturing Skills.

It is important to help an oral patient to develop self-nurturing skills and behavior if she is to heal deeply. The patient is asked to sit with her legs crossed. She creates a cradle with her arms and body. She is asked to see and hold her inner child that she has contacted in her previous work. She is instructed to tell her child that she will use the skills she has acquired in therapy, and as a grown up, to be a good parent to her child. Then she asks her child what she needs and wants. She then delivers on this request. If her inner child asks to be held, she holds her. If the inner child asks to be stroked, then she strokes her. The therapist suggests that when her inner child is needy, that the patient repeats this type of caring for her inner child. This can be a powerful intervention. It also helps the patient fulfill her need for deeper feelings of love and caring, as she provides this to herself.

The therapist will check on the armoring of muscles that she has worked in order to gauge the pace of the work. The patient checks in at the beginning of each session, so this report is another source for estimating the patient's progress.

Before the end of therapy, I review with the patient the friendships she has. She reviews these to see which ones are satisfying to her. She is supported in appreciating people who care for her and meet her needs and who accept her caring for them. She is also supported in ending relationships with persons who are self-absorbed and who cannot give or respond to her needs. It is pointed out to the patient that the longer-term relationships require reciprocity between her and her friends.

Additionally, it is important for patients to *eventually* face the reality that, now that they are grown up, they have to put out effort to get their needs gratified. This is an ego development that occurs later in the therapy, *after* the patient has worked through their anger and pain about being victimized.

Oral Patient's Narrative

[The following report is from a patient who has trained with me in ISP. Therefore, he uses body psychotherapy language. He can report very articulately on his experience in treatment. Most of this report is his narrative about his work. I asked him questions before he wrote his report. My comments about his writing are in brackets.

All patients are asked to keep a journal about their sessions in therapy and whatever came to them after their sessions. They do this journaling on the day of their session. This is done because so much of the work is body based. Doing the journaling helps patients to cognitively integrate their work.]

I started body psychotherapy with Jerry in July 1996. I was in the [ISP] training group and I remember going through an informal interview at lunch to convince Jerry of why I wanted to go into therapy with him. I told him that I had "scared myself" at a body lab [The Body, Self and Soul Workshop] in 1981 and now I was finally "ready" after my experience thus far in the training and from a body lab earlier this year. I was not afraid of Jerry but had fear of "what I may find out about myself."

[What did I want to get from ISP? This includes a statement of the problem.]

From my journal… "I want to live my life in a more congruent way with where and who I am. I want to simplify my life (e.g., get rid of things/stuff). I want to be more spiritual; I want peace and serenity.

I want to be more connected to both parents. I want to give more and get more from relationships. I tend to give more, and in the extreme, I will pull back and withdraw (e.g., in business, if I have done too much, then the next project I will procrastinate; with wife, I won't initiate sex.) I want more balance in my life."

I do not think that what I came into therapy to work on changed all that much over the course of my treatment; it just deepened. In truth, I really wanted a relationship with myself, to know myself on the deepest level possible. I had never allowed me to "go deep" and my body was the only access point where my relationship with me was going to happen. I avoided emotional pain with my Pollyanna attitude. It took me a considerable amount of time—years—to let go/give up my denial. My denial protected "the premature infant inside"…The numbness in my body, the lack of awareness of sensations, was profound. I remember with "awe and wonder" especially with the first several sessions of body therapy where I came alive. Energy was available to me. [He faces himself with his capacity to have more energy. It is crucial for him to see this early in his therapy.]

I came into therapy open, yet guarded. What became obvious was the impact of being born 2.5 months premature (incubators had barely been invented—1949); being in the hospital alone, longing for contact with my mother, and the lack of attachment/warmth. [Being born prematurely, and the separation from his mother at birth, initiates this patient's development as an oral character, since he missed mothering. That his mother was blind for several months after she gave birth also limited the mothering she was capable of giving then.]

My throat is tight/restricted and my breathing is shallow in the first phase of therapy. Some early images in sessions: 1: wrestling with a grizzly bear.... holding on to myself, wanting more nurturing and letting go at the same time to get new awareness/experience...realization that my parents and wife do love me. I roll on the floor in a playful way (self-nurturing). [The very beginnings of integration of positive/negative aspects of self, i.e., self-absorption and giving.]

2. Image of stomach eating my heart—I am angry at my overweight condition, aware that I am blocking both receiving and giving love.

3. Dream sequence where I am talking to/woman classmate (mom part of me). I talk on & on & on in session. Jerry brings me back to go deeper...I talk to my Mom from the premature infant part of me about how my coming into the world caused her temporary blindness and inability to have more kids. With tears, I express sadness and guilt.

What I wanted out of therapy as I said did not change, but deepened... this inner knowledge of self. I had phases of deepening into myself throughout my therapy experience. Some aspects were "surprises", i.e., coming to know what I did not know consciously. I became more in touch with inside energy as a guide as to what to do or not to do. Paying attention to my energy and then acting from that place happened in and out of the therapy room and still serves me well today. With awareness of my energy, I do not "give myself away" but act from what is "right" for me (even if others don't agree). For example, I work to put boundaries around draining parts of my experience (e.g., maintaining and organizing material items; anxiety about financial security), and thus feel an incredible amount of freedom (within boundary). [Helping this patient to de-armor by doing bodywork decreases his numbness, which helps him to increasingly become self-aware so that he can guide himself more fully in his life. He can be more autonomous, which is important for an oral. And his choices are based on authentic aspects of his self.]

In 1980 as an adult, I first told my father that I loved him. My mother became threatened that my father and I were getting close and even stated that she felt "left out." My father and I both "shut down" and did not pursue strengthening our relationship. In fact, I am painfully aware of how much energy it took to suppress and contain those positive feelings in order not to "hurt" my mother. In ISP years later, I expressed anger toward my father for his passivity and not being available when in reality I was behaving the same way. [He is able to confront himself, which establishes his autonomy more fully.]

Another way of saying what I wanted out of therapy, was Love—the ability to give and receive love (I am triggered by Jerry working my neck, chest and shoulders, all moving in the direction of my heart.) I have experiences of feeling my father's openness and feeling sadness that I closed my heart to my overwhelming mother (to protect me) and thus to my father as well (my body does not separate the two of them…yet). I have a dream of walking through a snowstorm and in feeling a deep coldness, I find my capacity to love. I rid myself of my mother bonds (the internal ones) and discover that I have an internal governor which will keep my energized efforts responsible and at the correct intensity.

An event at the end of my freshman year in high school deeply impacted my trust in my mother. My mother told me if I did not get on the honor roll in the last six weeks of school, then I would have to go to prep school. I usually "came through" for myself and others in "the clutch", and I did this time by getting on the honor roll. My mother did not trust that this would happen and sent a non-refundable deposit to the school. I was angry and openly expressed my anger including the statement, there is no way in hell I am going away to prep school!!! My father talked to me privately, acknowledged my mother's error and "made me a deal." "William, this is a lot of money to lose. If you choose to go, then no matter how you do, you can come back to public school when the school year is up." So, I went and did do well AND did decide to come back to public school. I believed this was fair and that my Dad was respecting me. Years later, I picked up my father from a weekend men's retreat that I had given him as a birthday present. On the way back we had the start of many meaningful, heartfelt conversations that continued on until his death. On that drive, my Dad made amends to me telling me that in actuality that he was changing jobs and wanted me to go to prep school so that I would not be pulled out of school mid-year when we would move. Because I was in ISP at the time, I was able to allow myself to be angry/hurt and express these feelings to him and within 10-15 minutes switch to feeling appreciative and being loved by him—he was taking care of me in the best way he knew. By experiencing and talking to my parents in ISP [with intense anger and then love], I was able to BE authentic in real life with my father and later, my mother. [He is almost aware of the shift in his feelings from anger to love that comes from his expressing and deeply feeling his anger: the paradox of change.]

The intensity my mother carried was expressed toward me by smothering behavior. With her tight hugs, I felt engulfed. She taught Algebra and I was flunking Algebra. She attempted to tutor me, was overbearing and critical. We would get in verbal fights that lasted "forever." She could not let me be separate from her. Her self-worth depended on how I did in Algebra. [His insight is very important for his growth.]

Later on, she confided in me the disappointment she experienced having sex with my father. This boundary violation was painful but I still listened. In truth, I did not want to risk the loss of her (my own attachment to her since she was not around for my premature birth), nor did I want to incur her wrath. I also sensed how fragile she was. This is an example of how I "gave up myself in service to her." In addition, I was starting to understand that she was chemically dependent.

Again, with ISP I experienced my anger, sadness, hurt in my body, and as encouraged, to express this directly to her in therapy (Gestalt-like), my experience of her. This externalization gave me the courage, power and freedom to do this in real life when I was ready, which I did. I did confront her about her chemical and alcohol use. She never stopped, which was sad. I, however, stopped taking responsibility for her and reclaimed my own life. I focused on my life—friends, relationships, meaningful work, hobbies and listening to my body about what I wanted.

My dependency for survival on my job—that at some point we (my business partners and me) would sell our consulting firm and I would have a pile of money in order to retire and feel "safe", and that I could have "enough". In ISP, my experiences over time informed me that I had become a workaholic, that my identity and ego were attached to my work and that I was feeling "trapped". I had images of being on a beach, flying in the sky while tethered to the earth. Living a passive, yet full life in Hawaii emerged. I eventually faced with courage the prospect of leaving my business with no guarantees of what was next. I grieved, was angry, sad, and appreciative of what I had created and felt the loss of it all, even before I left. So when I left, I was clean, I was clear, I was ready. I knew in my body, in my gut that I had the resources within myself to not only survive but to live my life more fully than ever. [He transcends his orality: workaholism to him is an (oral) addiction to being well fed and secure. He works in therapy to free himself of his addiction while he terminates from his consulting firm.]

Going back to being born over many sessions over a period of years has been THE KEY to appreciating my body, my emotions and my soul, all resources available to me. Being born premature was a choice I made. My mother's body/cells were attacking my body. I became aware that my back helped me to survive long enough to be born. My back protected me from her destructive cells, which could get to my stomach. My back helped me to hang on. In my therapy, the hard touches to back and front (both different in terms of tightness) helped my stomach and heart to "get to know each other". My stomach and heart became more open. My back was loosening, letting go and softening. In my previous experience I always needed to get my back up. I'd have to be ready all the time. I would have to lead with or from my back.

I came to KNOW in my body that I can lead more from my open heart which is soft, female even, and still be safe and protected even if my heart is open. My back will protect me. I need to have my back in my background. My back can back me up and support me. It does not need to take the lead. This tells me why my back has been tight for so long—protection focused. [His awareness of how his back has protected him comes to him from the work he does in therapy as his back de-armors. He moves himself out of his early rigid defensive stance to a more flexible, healthy one.]

I wanted to have more of a sense of freedom. How does this come about in therapy and in life? Spontaneously! The safety of the therapy room, Jerry and the ISP process enabled me to explore my inner depths, often effortlessly and/or in moving through my resistance. I begin to define freedom as having more energy, being more expansive and playing. I start to "let go" of an assumed belief/fear that I will run amok, be out of control and lose myself. I experience myself as calm and centered. White is my color of freedom; black is being encumbered and death. Freedom is pacing self slowly (image of an elephant). Risk taking becomes a pleasure.

I notice that expressing my anger increases my energy. Acceptance of my anger is connected to my ability to love more fully. My mother did not allow me to be angry. I came to be able to love my mother more as I allowed myself to be directly angry with her. I projected onto my wife that she would leave me if I got angry. The experiences in ISP allowed me to claim myself as a separate person, particularly from the women in my life. By moving from my passivity to be assertive, I regained or perhaps for the first time connected to my deeper self and I started to like who I am. [Notice how he has these insights emerge from himself. I suggest processes to him that help him to get crucial self-awareness. He "owns" his therapy.]

I have always had a sense of spirituality. Early in therapy I had ethereal "spirit" experiences in which I was not grounded—kind of "airy/fairy", not really connected to self. Slowly, I could feel "spirit within me" and I began to trust it. I was "lost" due to the terror, vulnerability, and abandonment I experienced in my premature birth. A major portion of ISP has been focusing on this early life experience enabling me to have spiritual experiences in and outside therapy.

My spiritual connection started in ISP when I did an INTENSIVE (therapy sessions of 3 hours each day for 5 days in a row, being in silence the remainder of the time). My therapist suggested the intensive since my body resistance (armoring) was keeping me in a "fog", not being connected to myself. I was in a vulnerable place and became aware of a "split" in me: my numbness, a head oriented way of being, contrasted with my growing awareness of sensations, and feelings in my body. Specific grounding interventions really helped me:

The Spread Eagle position is an extremely grounding position. The person is asked to spread their legs apart farther than their shoulders. Their feet point outwardly from their toes. Then to do a knee bend while their hands touch the top of their thighs with their thumbs on the inside. Their arms are held straight. They are asked to breathe deeply from their mouth and nose.

Again, they are asked to lower their upper body as low as they can.

They hold this position as long as they can. When they come up, they shake each leg out. I became aware of how much I endure with tolerating the pain in my legs and pelvis (pain in my life that I had been avoiding). I became aware that I had the power and control to STOP my pain by moving out of the position.

A series of hard touches to my chest and upper back enabled me to really breathe and feel really ALIVE. I became aware of how I have not known or allowed myself to breathe fully since I was born. My therapist commented on how full my breathing was and that in the past it had been very shallow. Up until that moment, I really was unaware in my own experience of how restrictive, shallow my breathing has been all my life, likely due to my premature birth. His comment alone helped to validate and reinforce my new experience of breath. These hard touches to my chest and upper back throughout my therapy, increasing my capacity to breathe fully, have given me access to bodily sensations and awareness of my energy flow. Later on in ISP, these hard touches produced pleasurable, nurturing feelings.

Eye Work – My therapist looked into my eyes, asking what I was feeling and told me to bring my feelings into my eyes, and then he said what feelings he saw in my eyes: verbally encouraging/giving me permission to experience these feelings MORE. This process produced in me a sense of validation of myself and knowing I am "being seen" by my therapist. A variation of this was my experience of his woman partner (in an intensive) where I could see myself reflected in her eyes (feelings of terror, sadness, acceptance, love, healing) which was profound in helping me to heal my "mother wound" in particular, my mother's rage and depression that I felt within me.

Soft Touch--to my back propelled me into deep sadness. The verbal instruction/permission to continue my grief by my therapist, his acceptance of me in this state and allowing as much time as I needed, helped me deepen my experience. He would often say, "Let yourself know if you are finished, and if not, continue.

Simultaneous Soft Touch—To my chest (heart) and neck really helped me stay in my body (and not go away) and gave me an internal experience of extreme calm and peace…and most important, SAFETY.

One aspect of the Intensive was getting up in the middle of the night and walking around outside in the silence and having an existential experience of being with and connecting to the world. I was not alone!

I became aware of the God in me really connected to me.

Other Spiritual Experiences—At 3 a.m. in Mexico while on vacation, I was alone and observed a burning fire (real) and found myself "pulled into the fire". I felt terror intensely and yet was mesmerized and in awe of a presence. I did not feel alone or abandoned. [This feeling of a "presence" gives him a deep connection to his soul; his early abandonment is transcended!]

Approximately 9 months before my mother died, my mother sat up in bed (she had Alzheimer's) with tears in her crystal blue eyes and asked me, "Have I been a good mother?" I said, "yes" and gave her some examples with tears in my eyes. Then I asked her, "Have I been a good son?" She said, "yes" and she gave me examples including that I was and had been compassionate with her. She then laid back down and was "gone again" never to communicate again. I have this be a profound spiritual experience. I believe that I never would have been able to respond to her in a genuine, authentic manner if I had not done my "mother work" in ISP. I allowed myself to be vulnerable with her in her vulnerability. I allowed myself to trust her and myself—all of which I had previously learned and experienced in ISP. This experience was totally new to me as a result of my therapy. [This is a spontaneous change in the patient, which is a shift that occurs from this patient doing his "mother work" going deep down into his feelings of anger towards his mother. He goes fully into his angry feelings towards her so that he goes into these feelings deeply and through them to his loving feelings towards his mother. This is an example of an important paradoxical change in him. And this is spiritual for him; it occurs during his mother's last consciousness.]

The most intense spiritual experience in therapy was seeing and observing my soul. It was this red sphere with a white streak running through it. When I saw it I was terrified and thought that I was "losing it." At the time I was reluctant to tell my therapist of my experience. However, I did and was validated by him. (Perhaps this was one of the last levels of deep trust coming about in our relationship…without my fear of criticism.) My therapist normalized my experience by saying, "You may experience things in therapy that you can not put into words or even know how to express." Jerry was also "matter of fact", was not negative or positive—which really helped me to fully accept what I was experiencing and not deny nor dismiss it. [Notice the flowing nature of the patient's experiences. They come out, as he is ready psychologically and somatically. To him they are his because they occur as he gradually goes deeper into his self and soul.]

CHAPTER 5

Treating the Anal Masochist

Etiology

The focal issue is the mothering person's attempts to control her child, which gets focused on toilet training. The mothering person has extremely high expectations for the child to be clean and that the child does as they are told. The neurological development necessary to control one's anal sphincter, so that they can be toilet trained, occurs, on average, at the age of two years. Mothers of anal masochists, with anxiety about cleanliness and with high control needs, start well before this age. There have been reports of initiating toilet training as early as six months of age. Such children are put into an extremely difficult situation. The mothering person who does this is oblivious of her child's capabilities. Such mothers may use enemas to exact obedience from their child.

These mothers intuitively know about the gastro-ileac reflex and often put the child on the toilet right after they have been fed, not to be removed until they produce feces. Toileting accidents are met by punishment and humiliation. These children grow up with a tremendous pressure to perform to get acceptance and approval.

The mother's position is to be critical of the non-performing child. The child grows up to be self-deprecating, as he internalizes his mother as an introject. These children push themselves to perform at extremely high levels of performance. Such a child grows up to be masochistic. He also can flip into living from his mother introject: he pushes and tries to control others. Thusly he may flip into a *sadistic stance*.

Usually the child fears being assertive, thereby avoiding disapproval or being humiliated. Therefore, he cannot let himself be overtly angry with his mother for her over-control and her criticality. The resulting character stance is spitefulness towards the mother and others who try to control him. Spitefulness gives very little relief of the underlying anger. Therefore, the masochist is locked in, exerting a lot of energy to suppress and repress their intense anger.

Somatic Aspects of the Masochist

Because they are so locked in, overall they are clumsy, muscle-bound, stiff, and less able to do fine muscle activities well. They favor doing large muscle activities.

Face, Neck and Shoulder Girdle

Their facial muscles are tight—their face looks dull.

Their throat is tight and they tend to whine when they talk. Their neck is short and thick. The shoulder girdle is armored—the shoulders are large—from holding back their rage at their mother—and from shouldering this great burden. They are barrel chested to protect their heart from their mother—their breathing emphasizes inhalation of breath more than exhalation. Their shoulder girdle is tight.

Pelvic Girdle

Their pelvic girdle is tight too. The tightness and armoring of the shoulder girdle and pelvic girdle reflect a tension going down from the shoulder girdle and up from the pelvic girdle. So the body is like a barrel under great tension and pressure. Their back is tight—they hold themselves *back*. They cannot fully feel their backbone—they lack courage. They do not trust others—out of a fear of being controlled.

Legs

Their legs are tight, too—so locomotion is limited. They are over-grounded because of their tight legs. When they walk, they lead with their chest and stomach.

A relevant descriptive metaphor uses car driving: they push their feet on the accelerator and brake at the same time. So they exert a lot of energy without a substantial effect. They feel physically rigid and in a morass or a bog. Their energy is kept in their core—they are over-contained. They are vulnerable to depression: they feel bogged down.

As they do things, they squeeze and pressure themselves to perform—sexually their pleasure is limited by having to push against their inner holding back. Orgiastic pleasure is limited by their anticipation of pain. In holding back the expression of their anger, the patient concurrently holds back softer, loving feelings.

The Therapy of the Masochist

Useful general principles are to reduce resistance (e.g., by doing deep tissue work on tight muscles), followed by soft, nurturing touch to increase the strength of impulses.

Apply deep pressure to the muscles of the neck, shoulders, and the long muscles of the back, followed by soft touch to these same muscles. Then supporting the patient to express their feeling more fully as they face their elicited introjects on a mattress before them. Initially they are also likely to take angry action towards these figures. These actions often lead to the finishing of traumatic experiences.

Breath work is initiated by using stress work (the backward bow followed by the forward arch) while breathing deeply. Then direct pressure to the chest can be used next.

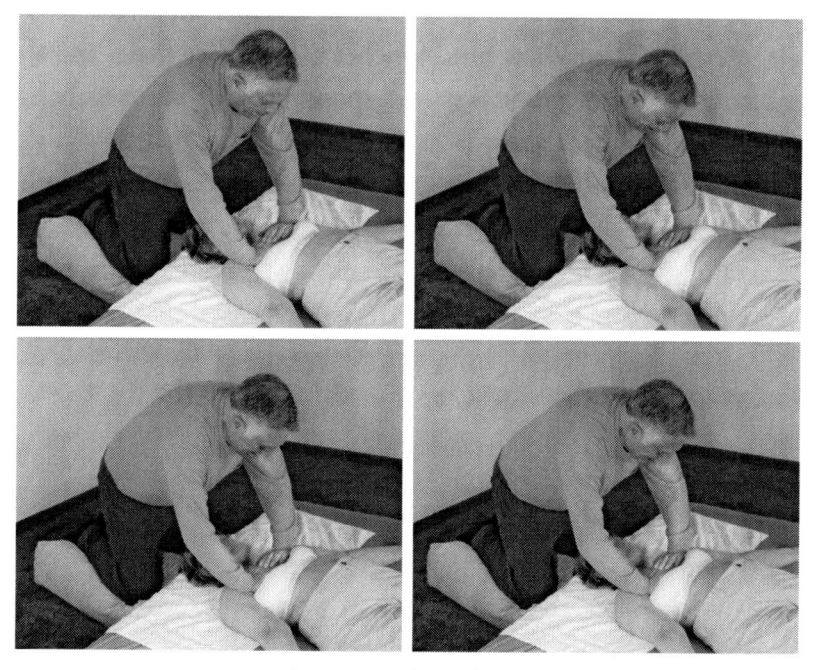

Ironing the Chest

Illustration 6. Ironing the Chest

This intervention increases the depth of the patient's exhalation of breath. The therapist uses her weight over her arms to make the touch deep. The therapist works on his chronically expanded chest. The patient is asked to stay in the supine position on the mattress. The therapist kneels at the head of the patient. She puts her hands on his chest, shaping her hands to fit his chest. Breathing with her patient, she comes up on her knees and uses her weight to deliver a pressured touch to his chest. Her hands face each other with her fingertips almost touching each other. Her fingers are extended so that there are no spaces between them. She touches him above his nipples--this positioning provides a broad coverage of his chest.

She does three touches on exhale. The therapist's first touch is more tentative, gauging the flexibility of his shoulder girdle. If the girdle is unyielding then the next two touches increase very gradually in their intensity. These three hard touches extend his exhale, and then his inhale increases gradually and spontaneously after each hard touch. If the patient's chest is more flexible at the first touch, then the therapist intensifies the strength of each of the next two touches. These chest touches likely elicit angry feelings and the therapist focuses on helping her patient to express any feelings that arise more intensely and more fully.

The therapist may then move on to a soft touch to the chest area.

Healing Body, Self and Soul

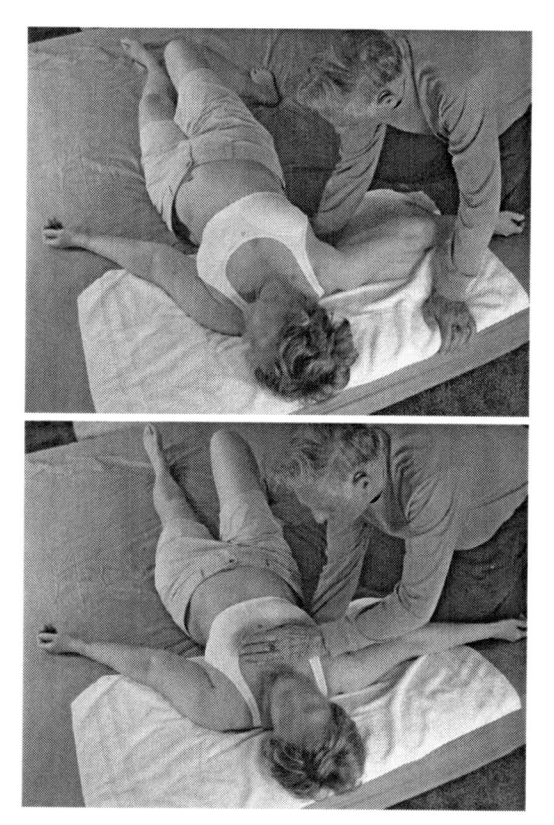

Holding His Heart Between Her Hands

Illustration 7. Holding His Heart Between Her Hands

The patient stays in a supine position on the mattress. The therapist gets into a supine position along side her patient. She places her left hand under her patient's heart. She shapes her hand to fit the contours of his back. Then she rolls onto her side and places her right hand on top of his heart. She has her right hand fit the contours of his chest/heart. She mirrors his breathing with hers. This is a powerful touch—to hold his heart between her hands. This touch likely elicits soft, loving feelings. And he can express these feelings or whatever else arises. The therapist supports the intense expression of these feelings.

Masochists are fearful of changing; they are exposed to being vulnerable, which is being soft. They have built a life of being tight and tough, so that the expected humiliation doesn't hurt them. They will not display their hurt from their anticipated fear of being shown to be lacking.

I had a masochistic patient who was adamant about seeing me only every other week. His muscles in his torso were massive and very tight. I worked to start releasing the muscles of his shoulders and back. He would express some feelings. Then in two weeks, when he came back for his next session; most of his released muscles were as tight as they were at the beginning of the previous session. I worked on and on like this for many weeks. I suggested that he see me every week again, but his answer was still adamantly, no. Therefore, I soldiered on several more weeks. I was met with the same pattern as before. I could not penetrate his armor physically and psychologically. I ended up terminating with him.

Some masochistic patients have a strong, self-sabotaging part of self that emerges during this work. It is difficult to reduce their resistance to opening up. There is more about this issue further on in this section with the patient that is presented as a masochist at the end of this chapter.

As these somatic interventions are applied and soften the patient, he will increasingly shift his predominant feelings from spite to anger, which is much more effective in reducing his angry feelings than spite is. This is crucial. This shift strongly indicates that the therapy is being successful. The expression of rage and anger reduces these residual feelings. As the patient expresses these backed-up feelings of anger, the patient will start recovering and gradually express more soft, loving feelings. This sequencing of expression is natural and occurs spontaneously.

Having patients bring the feelings of rage and love up into their eyes as they make eye contact with their therapist's eyes helps to deepen these feelings, which is important for the patient to finish with his anger and rage and to move on.

Doing the backward bow and forward arch helps to reduce the over-groundedness of the patient, as does jumping up in bare feet on a soft rug mostly using their feet to elevate themselves.

The loosening up of the patient that comes from their direct expression of anger makes them more *flexible* in their lives. And they deepen their relationships because their fear of being humiliated is very much reduced. These are important changes as the patient heals.

A **Therapist's** Narrative Of Psychotherapy with an Anal Masochist by Leighton Clark

Ray started therapy in ISP at the recommendation of a marriage therapist who intuitively knew that he "needed to get into his body." Ray's initial problem was "how do I get through my divorce?" After [many] years of marriage, he knew he needed to leave but was ambivalent about his attachment to his wife. He started therapy with beliefs such as "I am not enough," "I am a failure," and "nobody appreciates me." *Even though he had been in talk therapy most of his life, he continued to grapple with self-degradation.* Defining his identity and "becoming lovable" and accepted by women were his goals.

As this patient became aware of his body, various sensations (vibrations/energy) in his thick legs (feeling more grounded) produced an awareness that he was not solely responsible for his divorce and that his wife's unresolved issues [from] her childhood contributed to the dissolution of his marriage. He came to understand that the personal growth he had experienced and was currently experiencing actually created the need for him to leave her much like he needed to leave his mother. Although this awareness was new, it was somewhat frightening and uncomfortable and took several sessions before integration occurred.

In subsequent bodywork, Ray recovered memories of being abandoned by both parents in differing ways. In a series of sessions, he relived the experience as a four-year-old of his mother literally leaving him behind at their house when they moved (and later his father coming to get him). In therapy, his lack of attachment to his mother was becoming evident. Her dominance of him and lack of regard for him became deeply real to him and thus was overwhelming to him in the present. Alternating hard and soft touches to his neck, shoulders, chest and back would often produce immense despair in the form of deep sobbing. He would start sessions with whining about not being loved by his mother, his ex-wife, and his girlfriend. He would question what was wrong with him, and wonder why he was defective and unlovable.

Over time, he began (very slowly) to claim his place in the world (his birthright) and to trust himself. He had strong, nurturing relationships with men and got positive feedback about how he was a "good guy" and a good friend who connected well with the male friends in his life. He would often came into his therapy and talked about this feedback to hear himself declare—even convince himself—that he was a good person. He would then ask, "Why can't women see this in me?" He acknowledged over- compensating in an effort to please and take care of women in the hope that they would reciprocate and give him love. After a five-day ISP intensive group workshop, he became aware of how isolated and excluded he felt. He was depressed, even suicidal at times.

This was a turning point in his body therapy. I knew Ray had an enormous amount of pent-up rage inside of him and that even with bodywork he was resistant to even acknowledging it in a full way. He would talk about being angry with himself and his parents, but would not express that anger emotionally or physically. I told Ray at the time that his isolation was killing him. He responded that he should be taken care of and that in a passive defiant way he was going to wait for that special "person" (woman) to emerge who would care for him. He adopted an "I will show you" attitude by withdrawing in a passive-aggressive, even spiteful way with me and the world at large; and by engaging in help-rejecting complaining. [His whining is typical of masochism. His spitefulness is his indirect way of expressing his intense anger at his controlling and rejecting mother.]

I told him he was "stuck" and needed a breakthrough experience that he could own and claim as his in order to live life on his terms. Although Ray could talk from his head, he did not come from his experience—in his body. Instead, his body was severely armored, thus cutting himself off from awareness of his deep feelings of stubbornness, vindictiveness, and anger towards his mother.

Jerry Perlmutter, PhD

I sent Ray to the author of this book, Jerry Perlmutter, to do a five-day intensive. [This intensive consisted of 3 hours per day of body psychotherapy with the remainder of his day spent in silence at a retreat center doing journaling, exercise and meditation.]

<u>This is Jerry Perlmutter talking now.</u> The first day I started using stress work and touch work. It was obvious that Ray was defending himself from these body interventions by not breathing much and by keeping his muscles tense as I did touch work. [As a masochist, Ray resists working through his feelings, and this is likely done without his awareness.] During the second day, Ray again started defending himself against the bodywork. I remembered him saying that he did massage therapy earlier in his career. Therefore, I asked him to start touching himself where he felt that he needed this, and in a way that felt right to him. If there were touches he wanted to do that he needed help to do, he could ask me to help. Initially, he touched himself. Then he started asking me to help him do his touches. By the third session, he just asked me to do touches. Having him touch himself and ask me for help in touching himself gave Ray a greater sense of self-direction and control, and this reduced his resistance. This is so because Ray's mother has been very controlling of Ray from his early childhood to this day. So this is a crucial issue for him.

During this third session and during the fourth and fifth sessions, he got in touch with his intense feelings of anger and rage towards his mother because she did not show loving feelings toward him, "she was narcissistic". In addition, she tried to control him by

Healing Body, Self and Soul

expressing strong feelings of disapproval. [During the rest of his intensive, he expressed his strong feelings of anger as he evoked his mother on a mattress in front of him. His angry feelings were very intense. He realized that he has been very spiteful towards her instead of expressing his anger. He realized that he was not letting himself succeed in life so that he did not support his mother's standing as a successful parent.]

[Back to his regular therapist here.] Unconsciously, Ray was cutting himself off from these feelings in order to exact revenge on his mother. In response to touches to his neck, chest, back and under his rib cage, Ray became aware of images in his experience that contained the beginnings of insight. For example, he became aware of the image of his mother with her back to him reading a newspaper, not seeing Ray, and causing Ray to feel invisible. This awareness was the start of sessions that deepened Ray's awareness of his need to be seen. In his image of his mother, Ray was able to get her to "turn around and talk to me". Ray became more aware of his spite toward his mother—and others—but especially towards himself. He often directed his anger at his mother towards himself, which he was just beginning to own. He had been a "good boy" so, "Why doesn't my mother love me?" Often, after stress positions, out of frustration he would say, "But I am a good man!"

After working with his grounding and breathing, Ray's work shifted to focusing on his father. His awareness of his feelings of spite and anger towards his father came out of using his whole body to beat on a padded stool. Intense rage emerged because his father had died of a heart attack when Ray was a young adult and had left him with "that bitch," namely his mother. After telling off his father in anger, Ray collapsed onto the floor into deep sobbing and despair. He was grieving the loss of his father essentially for the first time. As a result, he became aware that he has maintained his connection to his father [by going into his father's line of work]. Subsequently, in his life, Ray has connected to a variety of safe men and developed a "composite loving father introject."

Because of ISP, Ray has a direct connection to sensations in his body, particularly access to energy now available to him. He became aware of his own assertiveness and power and has taken steps to change his life: he recently retired from [his father's line of work]; he has done some writing, ended the relationship with his girlfriend, and decided to move [far from his home]. His move is a huge life decision as he is taking responsibility for his life and intends to live on his own terms.

As Ray terminated ISP, he realized he had healed significantly, even if not completely. His decision to move… represents a major life change for him not in reaction to or for anyone else.

The patient expresses in his own words the impact of ISP and his courage to assert himself: "the act of calling my mother to say goodbye turns into an opportunity for her to abuse me with her snide derogatory comments in a sarcastic tone of voice. My realization: because my body is more full and

Healing Body, Self and Soul

open, I do not merge with my mother. The behavior remains hers. Her behavior communicates nothing. I am not informed about what displeases her, certainly not what she is actually feeling. In the past when I would internalize her hostility, rage, rejection and displeasure, being the recipient led me to crippling immobility and gross insecurity. Due to the lack of information, I was victim to her compulsive unconscious clubbing. My mother stole my life. F* her. The experience lingered in my body. I did feel slight sadness. My mother's behavior is about power. I have a sense but not a full understanding about how this is the method she used to bond me to her: bonding through abuse."

In his body, Ray reports, "My abdomen distends fully, my diaphragm lowers, my rib cage opens in three dimensions and my sacrum moves." This is in response to feeling connected to his body and accepting himself—being authentic. He falls asleep sooner with dreams that are more intense than previously. A dream he had, once he moved, included the image of himself as an infant with his back to himself (as he was holding himself from the back), which he could fully feel in his stomach and his heart (self-nurturing). This is his emotional response—being calm—in reaction to "other people's energy" when he is being authentic and people cannot or will not take in who he is and instead demonstrate reactive behavior to him. Although he did not state this explicitly, I would surmise that, for Ray, this is simultaneously an experience of feeling grounded and surprised. In an email communication from his "new home," Ray expressed that he has never felt as much relaxation in his muscles nor has he ever felt as safe (except in my office) as he does now. [Ray is still in his first stage of treatment. He stops therapy to move away. While he could work on his early trauma more extensively, it was important for him to move and he reports that it is having a salutary effect on him. This is an illustration of our stand that patients set their time of termination without an attempt by the therapist to influence him to stay in therapy longer. The patient "owns" their therapy.]

[His is a clear case of masochism. This is why we included him in this book, even though he did not go deeply into therapy. This major level of resistance occurs often in masochists.]

CHAPTER 6

The Treatment of the Schizoid

This character is based on a fixation at the *visual phase* of development (0 to 6 months). This is the first stage of development. Freud did not identify this as a psychosexual stage. He started his scheme with the oral phase. Reich formulated this first stage. Hence, as Reich did, I also name this the *visual phase*.

Etiology

This fixation happens during the first six months of life as the infant looks at his parent(s) and sees rage in their eyes directed at him. The infant feels terror and ensuing coldness. The trauma occurs repeatedly in early childhood as the child "upsets" his parent(s). The parent(s) defend against feeling this rage so that it mostly remains unconscious. The child feels terror, coldness and numbness. These reactions of the infant are pervasive due to the intensity of the parent's feelings and the young age and the limited development of the infant. The child armors in their eyes, and this leads to a block between his head and body. This is the body split (schism) referred to in the name of the character: *schiz*oid.

Schizoid Body Structure

The Head

The *face* is mask-like from the armoring of muscles in the face. This reduces connection with others, not letting others in by minimizing facial cues. The person does not let his reactions show as a way of protecting himself from "life's dangers." His eyes look large and "shocked," or dull and deadened. Reich called the latter, "going away in the eyes".

Splitting of the Head from the Body—The scalp is tight. The head is not firmly attached to the body. The head is pulled out, and the muscles of the neck are tight, especially at the base of the skull.

The head sits at an angle. This splitting of the head from the body is the somatic underpinning of the split between feelings and thoughts; i.e., emotionally intense thoughts are accompanied by flat affect. There is an absence of joy, not gloominess, but coldness or frozenness.

Again, there is a lack of expression in the eyes, or they are frozen in terror. The armoring of the eyes is the somatic aspect of the repression of his intense anger at his parent who expressed hatred and rage at him through their eyes. His voice is flat. His feelings are *blunted*.

The Body

His shoulders are tight. The arms are powerful but stiff and split from the body. Their movement is mechanical; the arms move like a windmill. His scapula is immobile. Tension in his pelvic hinge creates intense lower back pain. Muscles in the body, especially the back, are spastic but not armored. Anger at the angry, raging parent(s) is held in his muscles, especially his back. These feelings are unconscious. His soft muscles in the front of his body open him to feel empathy and tenderness towards others. There is little freedom of movement at the hip joint; his pelvis is immobile.

The body is not integrated with its action; the person does not identify with his body's movements.

The musculature in the front of the trunk is not spastic as the back is. This greater openness supports the experience of softer, tender feelings towards others. The schizoid is able to feel empathy, love and perhaps, spirituality.

Breathing

His diaphragm does not descend; it is frozen in a contracted position because of the terror experienced early in life. His curtailed breathing leads to a sapping of his energy. The frozen diaphragm leads to a division at the waist between the upper and lower halves of his body. Thus he disassociates from his sexuality.

Legs

The ankles are inflexible. The arches of the feet are weak. He is not grounded.

Jerry Perlmutter, PhD

The Therapy of the Schizoid

Overriding Issues

These patients seek psychotherapy because they are unable to develop relationships with others, or they are not successful at work.

Generally, they have a core of warm feelings, and crippled motor systems for discharge or expression of these feelings. They use their heightened sensitivity to avoid danger and in attempts to achieve success. They do not experience much success because of their limitations. The dilemma is what to do with their assertive, aggressive tendencies. These feelings are held back in the muscles. If their anger becomes conscious, they could get murderous. They are terrified of their hatred and anger, so they resist attempts to thaw out their muscles.

They lack ego defenses. They freeze in situations they see as negative or as dangerous to themselves. They are not armored. This is why I talk of their freezing, of their holding feelings in their muscles. Their ego is quite weak.

Treatment Interventions

The therapist starts at where the patient presents feelings: their social and work limitations. She explores the presenting problem to help him make it much more specific. The therapist reflects back the patient's feelings so that he experiences and owns these feelings. Eventually this increases the strength of his ego, i.e., his capacity to experience his inner life and, eventually, his capacity to take action. The reflection of the feelings back to the patient also initiates the formation of an important bond between the patient and therapist.

Then she moves to increasing the patient's low level of energy. She uses the backward bow and forward arch as a part of this effort. The therapist works to deepen the patient's shallow breathing which also increases his level of energy. The patient experiences more warmth, and this is important. She proceeds gradually.

Eventually patient action ensues from the build-up of energy. She utilizes the Awareness Cycle to increase the patient's identification with and ownership of his inner experiences and actions. She supports the patient in noticing the kinesthetics of his movements, so he gets an awareness of what his body is doing in space. Her aim is to increase his ownership of his movement, which is a way of helping him to deepen the foundation of his ego.

The therapist helps the patient to produce expressive movement by having them notice and expand the smaller movements they make spontaneously. She supports him in making sounds as he moves. This helps him to use his body more and to loosen up his muscles that have been held so tight. His emotions also emerge more as he does expressive movement. His capacity to experience pleasure is enabled. In this way he increasingly develops relationships with food, clothing, work objects and love objects. These help to fill out his ego. She uses deep touch on the muscles of his neck, shoulders and the back, followed by soft touch to these muscles.

She then addresses his eye block. She uses loose arm and body-swinging exercises to ease into the eye work gradually. The patient allows his head to swing too with his eyes open. This intervention relaxes his eyes, which counters his frozen, terrified look. When the patient is ready for more focused and catalytic work, she does the Eye Opener.

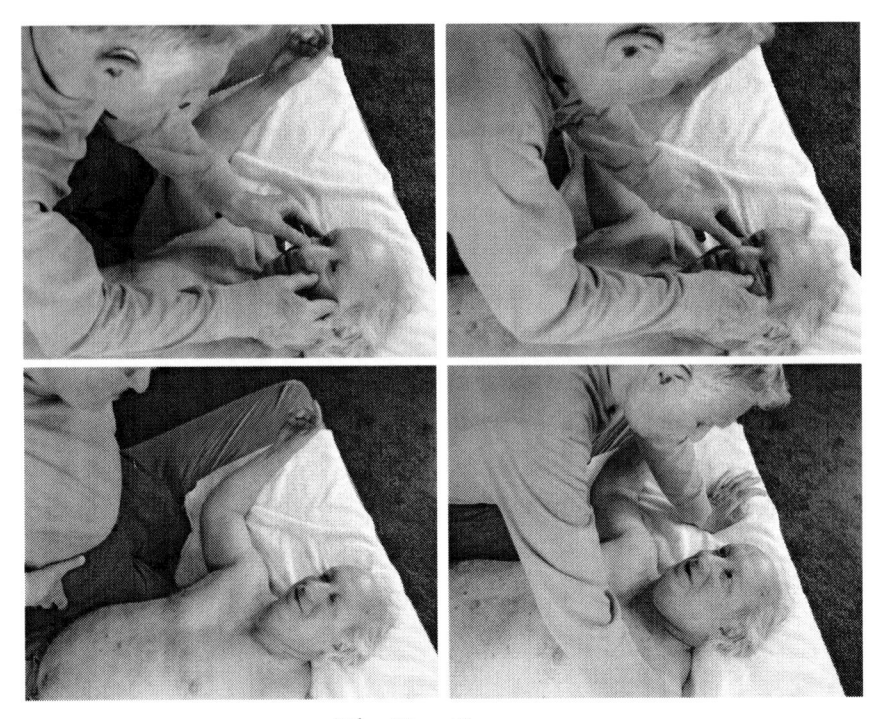

The Eye Opener

Illustration 8. The Eye Opener

The patient lies down on the mattress in a supine position. The therapist hovers over her patient with her head close to his so that she sees into his eyes. She places her hands near his eyes. Her thumbs are placed below his eyes on the bones there. Her index fingers go into the depressions on the bones on the sides of his eyes. She tells her patient to take a deep breath and she takes one, too at the same time. She brings her eyes close to his and stares at him as she applies deep touch with her thumbs and index fingers. At the end of their breaths, she ends the touch, but maintains eye contact. She asks him to bring his feelings into his eyes. Then she asks him to say what he is feeling. After he is finished telling her, she tells him what feelings she sees in his eyes. Then they process his experience. After this she moves on to a comforting touch.

Healing Body, Self and Soul

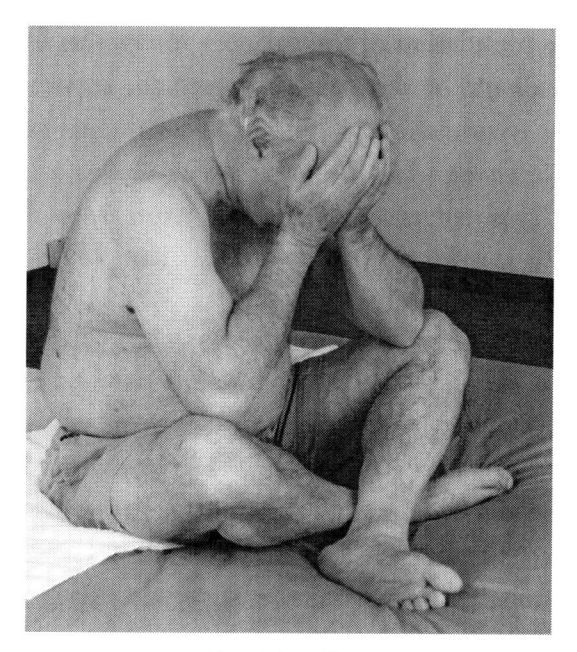

Eye Comfort

Illustration 9. Eye Comfort

The therapist helps her patient to sit up on the mattress. He crosses his legs and leans his elbows on his thighs. He bends his head forward and places his hands on his eyes so that his palms and arms support his head. He breathes deeply and notices what he experiences He holds this posture until he is ready to straighten his head and open his eyes. Then the experiences are processed (using the Awareness Cycle). The armoring of the eyes primarily involves the eye's extrinsic muscles.

She works on the tightness in his legs and the collapse of the arches of the feet. The side-to-side movement and the side-to-side stress positions help to heal these body limitations.

A schizoid patient's current relationships are based very much on transference-based projections. This happens because the traumas occur so early in the patient's life that the personalities of the parent(s) form the sole foundation of the patient's interactive life. Therefore, the therapist should be ready to *often* work the transference aspects of his present relationships. We assume that the patient must work parent transferences when he deals with persons who are in his current life. This extensive transference work helps the patient to externalize his introjected parents and to have fuller relationships with people in his life today.

The patient is supported to externalize his parental introject(s) by expressing his stored up anger at her, him or them, while he visualizes them on a vertical mattress before him. This also allows him to become physical with them by pounding their elicited image or stroking them etc. This externalization reduces his self-destructiveness immensely because he stops harboring intense anger that he has directed at himself. He becomes more self-accepting and more at peace with himself as he expresses more of his anger towards his parents. When these feelings of anger are sufficiently experienced and expressed, the patient often spontaneously shifts to expressing softer feelings at the parental introject: again, *this is paradoxical change.*

The ego building that is done early in the therapy, as outlined above, helps him to be more alive and present in his body. He is enabled to take directed action to express his feelings, and to get him more of what he wants and needs.

A Schizoid Patient's Treatment Narrative

[Why did you come into therapy with me? --what kind of issues did you have? Did your reasons to be in therapy change as you worked with me?]

Five years prior to starting ISP, I (Thomas) had left my professional career to "find myself". I thought that if I didn't have to spend so much time working I could untangle the problems in my life. Over the next five years, I engaged in a number of workshops, which emphasized self-discovery through breath and bodywork, gestalt therapy and group work. These programs were beneficial to me. However, at the end of each program, I slipped back into old patterns. I didn't possess the strength and will necessary to continue the transformation outside of the intimate and safe setting provided in the workshops. I had too much fear and resistance to do the work on my own. I was used to my habituated state of limited breath, isolation and deadness. That state was tied to my identity and on a primitive level, my very survival.

When I first learned of ISP, I quickly signed up for the upcoming ISP Soul Workshop. This was a life-saving event for me. I entered the workshop in an extremely constricted and depressed state. By its conclusion I had emerged with a strong determination to own and transform my life. The private ISP sessions that followed continued where the workshop left off.

Entry Issues

I was dealing with a long list of issues. I had been in multiple dual relationships for seven years, but couldn't decide whether to end or fully commit to any of these. This quandary tormented me and kept me from pursuing or committing to anything else in my life. My fragmented relationships were highly unsatisfying, yet I was at a loss as to what to do and I was obsessed with sorting it out. It was this conundrum that had led me to resign from my job and kept me from committing to any other full-time job. I had no idea what I wanted to do. I obtained some sense of meaning by caring for an ill family member, but this role did not last forever. I felt trapped inside and didn't know how to move forward. I had little confidence in myself. Internally I felt lost, lonely and isolated. There was no sense of passion in my life. I felt something was missing. Home was missing. Security and love were missing. Mama was missing. I was missing. [Follow his statements in reverse from Mama was missing and likely, you have a causative sequence.]

As an individual, I had a lot of fear. I had a great fear of failure and not being good enough. I had thoughts that I should have not been born and that I should have thrown myself from the crib. I was afraid of others. On some deep level I was terrified that I would be attacked and killed. [In earlier breath work there were periods of regression into a paranoid state, not trusting anyone.] I was unable to stand and take my own place. I was afraid to step forward and lead. I would abdicate authority to anyone who I deemed to be equal or superior to me. I felt worthless.

I was coping with my sense of emptiness through alcohol, television and pornography. My life was wasting away. I did not fully appreciate the magnitude of the obstacle that my fear and self-hate had created.

Through ISP I hoped I could find freedom, passion, meaning and direction. Additionally, I was interested in exploring the recesses of my subconscious. I had touched into dark energies of my body/mind at the core of my being which left me wondering if I was possessed or evil.

I will share one of those experiences here: I had an unusual experience during a breathing session with my "work" partner, Michelle, in which I regressed to an infant state and cried for a long time. My breathing and body movements matched the infant state. I was in intense distress. Through stroking a pillow, I seemed to tap into even deeper sadness and an unmet need for touch.

I observed myself in this state to try and understand the cause of the distress. All I could see was darkness. I regressed to lying in a crib crying in that darkness. I was inconsolable. As my breathing progressed, it vacillated between deep belly breathing and hyper, short upper-chest panting. I began to experience intense contractions in my arms and legs. I was lying on my back and rocking slightly with my arms extended tensely upward and my legs drawn up in a fetal position. It felt like a state of terror and protection. [He has regressed to being an infant in a crib. What follows in this section is initiated by this early regression. My interpretation, based on later work Thomas did, is that as he cried in the crib, if his father came in, his father was extremely angry at infant Thomas. Likely Dad's anger included his intense expression of his feelings in his eyes. This is the schizophrenic core trauma!]

I remained in this position and cried for several minutes. Finally Michelle took hold of my arms and legs as she asked me to release the weight of my limbs to her. I would partially release and then contract again, afraid to let go. Eventually my arms and legs collapsed by my sides. My sobs intensified, but it was now a sobbing of release as the terror had passed.

Next my legs and arms began to tense in rhythmic contractions and I howled an irritated cry. Michelle swaddled me in blankets to see if that would relieve my distress. However, I became filled with hate. It was as though a steely ice cold energy moved through my body from my feet to the top of my head. My cries shifted to cold hatred.

Michelle quickly removed the blankets and sat next to me. Energy moved through my body and into my right arm. My right arm raised itself and its fingers contorted above my face. With a tight mouth and contorted face, my mouth spoke and my hand and fingers moved like a puppet as I spoke the words:

> "I am the devil… I am what you are afraid of…I am the devil and have been inside you from the beginning…You are terrified of me and should be…I

am inside you and other people in your family too—
your uncle, your grandmother, your father..."

This was followed by repeated demonic laughter with my face contorted in an evil grimace. I watched all this, surprised, curious and a bit scared. [Notice his detachment from these experiences, which reflects the schizoid split of his head from his body. The pathology in this person was very great. ISP does not just deal with neurotic patients. ISP treats persons who have had massive amounts of trauma.]

Dual Relationships

Entering ISP, I was entangled in dual relationships. I had met Sarah, the first of my partners, many years earlier. She had come to me in desperation. She was penniless and in poor health. In meeting her, love and compassion entered my heart and I thought I should marry her. This was the heart connection that I had sought from my mother and the answer to my mantra "I want to be seen". Also, to me her dependency meant she would never leave me. She was what I had wanted my mother to be.

Unfortunately, I was not physically attracted to her and she failed to respect any of the boundaries that I set for myself. She made sexual advances, which reminded me of the sexual abuse I had suffered as a teenager and this generated sexual aversion. She wouldn't stand on her own and chose to be financially dependent on me. After three years I decided to leave the relationship to reclaim my autonomy. I moved away physically, but my heart stayed with her. We continued to carry on a long distance relationship. [The relationship he wanted with Sarah was non-sexual; there were strains of a Madonna/mother theme in it. He avoided acting on the Oedipal-sexual relationship with his mother. Sarah continued asking him for sex. Her pressure set limits on the relationship for Thomas.]

Healing Body, Self and Soul

Upon moving, I quickly entered into a new relationship with Becky. This was based on physical attraction and was a sexual relationship, but was void of a depth of heart. We dated for four years but due to my lack of connection with Becky I also wanted to leave this relationship. Every time I tried, a tremendous fear of abandonment would drive me back. While I remained in relationship with Becky, I continued to carry on a long-distance heart relationship with Sarah.

I moved yet again and began dating Michelle. With this new relationship in place, I disengaged completely from Becky. My sense of security, my very sense of survival was now tied to Michelle with whom I had a sexual and intellectual connection. However, she too didn't touch my heart as Sarah had. I did not feel seen by her in the wounded depths of my being. Additionally, I resented that Michelle was in contact with an old boyfriend of hers. This triggered my fear of abandonment. I wanted to leave but I couldn't let go. After seven years, we mutually agreed to end our relationship but terror arose in me. I begged her not to leave and she took me back.

Shortly after my last ISP sessions with Jerry my relationship with Michelle ended with the beginning of a new one. Still, my heart connection with Sarah remained.

I had unknowingly pieced together a puzzle of relationships, with one relationship partner (Sarah) representing an idealized symbiotic union, which threatened my autonomy, and others (Becky & Michelle) representing my conflicted dependent relationship with my actual mother.

The frustration and anxieties that I had experienced with my mother were being repeated in my adult relationships. In ISP the anger and hatred that I had repressed for so long finally burst. Becky, Michelle and my mother were together in my mind and I was filled with hatred.

While ISP did not release my relationship indecision and paralysis, Jerry offered this sound advice, "when there isn't an answer with the available information to make a decision (such as in my relationship dilemma) the only answer is to let go and go inside... breathe, experience and let things emerge from your body--open, experience life. There is no need to search for answers. They will emerge on their own, eventually in the right order of time." I have taken this advice to heart.

[How has your relationship been with your mother--trace the changes over time.]

MOTHER:

Our family lived an isolated existence away from a large city. My mother has not shared much from her childhood, but I have learned that her mother (my grandmother) was an alcoholic. My grandmother was unhappy, emotionally abusive and would not speak to my mother for days at a time as a form punishment. Needless to say, my mother learned to keep quiet. She carried that pattern into her relationship with my father and ended up not standing up for herself or her children.

As a child, my mother's sense of security was grounded in her father. She told me that she would stay up at night waiting for her father to pull into the driveway. She was worried that he would die on the road. She clung to the safety of her father as I had clung to the safety of my mother. Her father was afraid of his wife just as my mother ended up being afraid of her husband. The patterns had repeated.

As an adult, she carried this past trauma forward in the form of fear and self-doubt. She hid her feelings and thoughts. She stifled her brilliancy, laughter and joy. This was the soup in which I developed. And, so, I exhibit many of the same traits.

Healing Body, Self and Soul

My mother was burdened with five children, isolated in the country even though she had grown up in the city. I was born the third child. My mother cared for her two young toddlers while she was pregnant with me. Then news that her father was terminally ill undoubtedly caused my mother and me great distress while in utero.

Regarding my infancy, my mother said that I cried incessantly with "colic" and refused to eat. When I asked her if she breast-fed me, she responded, "I don't think so". She lowered her head after saying this, so I wondered if this was true. Based on a somatic experience that occurred toward the end of ISP therapy, but outside of the therapy setting, I came to believe that she did breast feed me for a short period of time before abandoning this in favor of a bottle.

I wanted to explore this aspect of my infant / mother relationship. So, outside of the ISP setting I asked my partner, Michelle, if I could suckle at her breast. She agreed, and I entered into a deep, soothing, infantile experience. After some time, Michelle became emotionally uncomfortable and pulled away asking me to suckle on a pacifier in place of her breast. My infantile self turned away. I felt willful hatred. My chin was drawn inward. There was a gaunt, emaciated look on my face like that of a concentration camp survivor. There was no going back. I wanted nothing to do with her or her pacifier (which represented a bottle to me). [Thomas has this be a reenactment of his being weaned from the breast by his mother, of being pushed away by his mother.]

The malnourishment, which came from my refusal to eat was with me throughout infancy and childhood. In grade school my parents took me for medical tests to determine if there was a physiological basis for my condition. The tests came back negative, but demonstrated the level of concern of my parents and doctors. Taking in nourishment remained an issue going forward until college.

Jerry Perlmutter, PhD

Looking back, my colicky screams seem to have been cries for help, nurturance and connection. Mother attempted to stop my crying, so I didn't feel authentically seen by her. At times I was simply left to scream and cry myself to sleep. My internal mantras, "See me" and "don't abandon me" were left unfulfilled. [This is likely the psychological core of his colic and "malnourishment".]

The environment at home was quite unpredictable for me as a screaming infant. I have bodily memories of highly traumatic physical and emotional attacks. There are no clear images of who may have participated in this. All I know is that I have relived these experiences through the memories stored deep within my body. These events set in place a foundational post-traumatic terror in my psyche. [Later on he says, there were times when my father was angry toward my mother for attending to my cries when I was in the crib. His father got intensely angry with Thomas. His father's anger from the competitiveness between him and Thomas is described in the next three paragraphs. I speculate that his father's anger at Thomas also occurred when Thomas was an infant in his crib, and that his father's anger had a visual component. This might have been a core schizoid-forming experience.]

This childhood emotional neglect led to an insecure anxious attachment with my mother. I was fixated on her for my safety and existence. Her unexpected absences activated terror and paralysis in me. I turned to no one else for support. When she did return, I was relieved and then resentful. However, I did not outwardly express this resentment. This attachment remained with me in childhood, adolescence and young adulthood until it was transferred in my adult relationships to my female partners.

Clinging to mother contributed to the formation of a triad between my mother, father and myself. The relationship with my mother became intricately tied to my father. As a small child I was jealous of my father and was deeply hurt when I was told I could no longer spend any time with them in their bed. I wanted to be close to her.

Once, I remember she was vulnerable and shared with me some of her fear and sadness around an illness she was experiencing. My father came into the room with a scowl on his face and asked what she was doing. She stopped. She seemed to be afraid of my father and received little support from him. On some level she used me as a surrogate. [Mother supports his Oedipus Complex.]

In childhood, I clearly had an active oedipal attachment to my mother. My father had little positive involvement in my life. All of my energies were directed toward my mother. Since my oedipal desires were naturally frustrated, I developed a love/hate relationship with her. [This frustration is a source of his later resolution of his Oedipus Complex.] There was no male figure available for positive relations and support.

During an ISP session, this Oedipus Complex played itself out in epic proportions from deep breathing. [I did touch work to his back.] I opened to my internalized mother. The hate buried for so long rose to the surface. I wanted her with all my might. I was lying on the ground yelling at her as she was leaving. I couldn't have her. I was filled with hatred. I grabbed a towel, which represented her. I squeezed and twisted it until she was dead. Unfortunately this outward display of emotion did not help alleviate my conditioning. I asked myself "Now what?"

As therapy continued, and as the pressure of my buried angry feelings were deeply expressed repeatedly towards my mother, my hatred suddenly shifted. In a very empowering ISP session, I lay on a mattress and spoke with my mother telling her of my love for her and that I wanted her to be free and happy. [After Thomas fully experiences his intense anger for his mother, and "kills her", he moves on spontaneously to a loving place with her. This is a transformation from the paradox of change: it occurs to him spontaneously.] I expressed my own autonomy and wholeness. I wanted the same for her. I felt love, appreciation and a strong desire for her happiness. This brought deep peace to me.

Shifting my internal relationship with my mother elicited a dramatic movement in my stance from that of a collapsed, powerless and dependent individual to a fully embodied, grounded and autonomous one. Until this movement occurred I would continue to drift through life in an infantilized state looking for a mother surrogate to provide self-definition and support. ISP began the process of this transformation.

FATHER:

My father grew up in the country with one younger brother. His father (my grandfather) was small in stature but commanding in respect. His focus was on growing his small business and saving every penny. He had little compassion for Grandmother. My grandmother had a deep faith, which was the center of her life. The joy of her life was cooking and serving food to others. Both of my Grandparents were strong willed. My grandfather expected my grandmother to serve him and she expected him to live as she thought he should. There was frequent conflict between the two of them.

My grandparents' lives were difficult during my father's youth and they spent little time attending to their children. My grandmother acknowledged to me that she showed little love to her children and that they basically raised themselves. My grandfather used a strong hand with them and expected a lot from his boys. This upbringing undoubtedly conditioned the views of my father.

Between the two brothers, my father was treated with more respect and privilege. This continued through to adulthood. My father seemed to have it all, while his brother had little.

I had a conflicted, passive-aggressive relationship with my father. As stated earlier, there was a triad between my mother, my father, and me. My father bristled when I sought my mother's attention from my collapsed and dependent stance. His disregard for me would show at the dinner table when he would belch, hold the air in his cheeks, turn toward me and then blow in my face. I hated this yet never even considered opening my mouth to speak up.

My father held few positive roles in my life. He didn't play with me, guide me or teach me. Most importantly I did not feel loved or valued by him. As an adult, one of my older brothers asked my father why he hadn't been more involved in our lives. He replied, saying, "one day your mother asked me to take you and your brothers on an outing, but it didn't work out." We disrupted his fun, so he never took us along again. He was focused on himself and his desires, but not on his children.

My father embraced the role of disciplinarian. He punished me, and my siblings with a stick to keep us in line. However, his most effective form of punishment was shame. Sadly, the punishments were never followed by love or affection. A few years ago my father commented saying "The only thing I did wrong as a father was that I was too lenient upon you as children."

As we got older, my father assigned outdoor projects to me, and my brothers, but he failed to provide any instruction. Within himself, he could see his desired outcome, but he never shared any of the "how" with us. We were left wondering what to do. We tried, but the results were never good enough for him. Seeing the results of our efforts, he would humiliate us saying, "What are you a stupid idiot? Get out of the way. Do I have to do everything myself?

Growing up in such an environment was demoralizing. There was no safe way to express my feelings. As a result, I internalized my anger and hatred. I hated myself and displayed passive aggression toward my father. "Fine, if you think I'm useless, then I am useless. I will prove you right." There was a part of me that didn't want to succeed because I thought this would reflect well on him. In the end, his constant humiliation and dismissal of my personhood led to feelings of worthlessness. I became afraid to try anything. I learned to hide. I was essentially dead. The irony in all of this was that every once in a while, he would say to someone, "Thomas has such potential if he would only try".

My dad subconsciously came to represent God to me. He was a strict moralist. He held firm views of the world including the trappings of righteousness and punishment, declaring that we would go to hell if we didn't comply. By my nature I was and am a curious individual and internally questioned what my parents' and their church taught. It didn't make sense to me. At the same time, I deeply internalized the messages and thought I was damned. On an emotional level, I didn't respect my father and I didn't respect God. My anger toward my father became anger toward God. During one ISP session my bitter hatred for God boiled over. I was ready to choose hell over a God who created and allowed such injustice. I was possessed by my hatred in a standoff with God. No direct resolution of this internal conflict occurred during ISP. Thankfully it did eventually resolve through my deepening spirituality.

My father also carried a great deal of sexual shame. He was absorbed by the teachings of his religion as passed on by his parents. His sexual shame became my own. If anything of a sexual nature appeared on the television, he would yell at us saying, "Do you want to watch that?" I simply looked down in shame. Internally I thought, "Of course I want to see that." The message that developed was: "I am bad for being sexual." My own sexuality became disconnected from my heart and lead to a distorted and dysfunctional sexual history.

During ISP sessions my internalized father was a frequent focus of attention. When facing him; hatred, anger, rage and violence would arise from my depths. There was so much contempt for him. Over and over again I stood against him by yelling out or taking a stance in silence to guard against him. My anger and willfulness were so great it seemed I would never get through it.

In one ISP session I confronted my father and screamed, "GET OUT, F* YOU!! LEAVE ME ALONE." I could feel hate rise up within me. I became powerful. Our roles were reversed and I dominated him. Jerry encouraged me to take my place and stand firm. [I was a cheerleader for him] I was here fully alive. I blew on my father. He turned to smoke and disappeared.

A second ISP session proved transformative. I confronted my father telling him not to touch me. I felt hatred toward him emanating forcefully from my left eye. Jerry told me to pull the hate out of me. I reached up and began to pull the hate out of my eye with my hands, as though I was pulling on a <u>rope or a snake.</u> It seemed like I was pulling a demon from me. [This is an example of concretizing a metaphor--this is discussed in Chapter 9. His hate is embodied as a snake in his eye. Removing the snake from his eye frees him up.] I kept at it until I sensed it was removed and then I cast it aside and turned away to face my internalized father again. I separated myself from him declaring "I won't collapse; you collapsed. I choose love; you chose hate. I choose compassion; you chose condemnation. I choose openness, you chose to be closed." [I asked Thomas to see his evoked father on the mattress and tell him how he was different from his dad. In systems theory, it is differences that form boundaries.

Feeling his boundaries with his father helped him to bound and externalize his father-introject.] In that moment a shift occurred. I realized that I was the one who had turned away from my father. [As Thomas deeply experienced and expressed his feelings of anger, he was able to spontaneously shift beyond these feelings to his grief and compassion for his father. This is the paradox of change. Notice all of the healing Thomas has in this session.] I recognized that I had punished him. I had not loved him. [As patients work on their feelings in ISP, I have them say to a parent—I have the father part of me, hating me.] I sobbed and apologized to him. I turned to my left and saw a vision of humanity. I felt all of the suffering and all of the pain in the world. I was overwhelmed and overcome with sadness, grief and compassion. [As a schizoid, his deep feelings of love emerge from the soft front of his body.]

I turned toward Jerry to give him a hug. In that instant he represented my father. I cried exclaiming, "I'm sorry, I'm sorry." It was healing. I had a felt sense of connection and love for my father. I could see my own role in choosing to turn away. I began to take ownership of my part of our relationship!

My relationship with my father has continued to improve post ISP. I am seldom intimidated by him. I am much more confident in myself and in my abilities. I disengaged from his guilt filled religious stories. The beliefs of my father have no benefit for me and I have left those with him.

With the support of Jerry and the ISP setting, I stood and confronted the father part of me and the mother part of me, both aspects which had been catalysts for my collapse. I declared my space and my body to be mine. I claimed my place in the world in a dramatic and authentic way. This was not role-playing. This was a full-bodied healing experience emerging organically from my body and mind. [Yes, this is healing!]

The true impacts of some of these transformative sessions were not fully felt until I left the session room. It was then that I noticed how expanded my energetic body had become. I radiated far beyond my physical body. I was strong and powerful with a determined will.

This shift into expanded presence was not a permanent state. I returned to the familiar habituated state as time passed, but I was gradually opening to a life more alive than I had known possible. This was redeeming in that it demonstrated to me the capacities that are inherently mine.

Are you able to work yourself now that you are no longer in ISP?

[This is a postscript to Thomas' ISP psychotherapy.]

> Three years after the start of ISP therapy and prior to our final meeting, I attended a workshop in which over several days the question "Who Am I?" was deeply contemplated. In a flash of time, I experienced myself as pure awareness. I was awareness prior to thoughts, emotions, bodily actions and sensations. These were all objects within my conscious awareness. My definition of "self" was permanently changed in that moment.
>
> The discovery of this "awareness as the ground of my being" freed me in two ways. First, my obsessive struggles to fix my life all but stopped. I saw what my obsessive thoughts really were, a dead end of madness. Now my life's direction comes to me spontaneously. Second, this stable awareness has provided a tremendous support for my internal exploration. [Probably this awareness work is based, in part, on his work in ISP with the Awareness Cycle,

and from having him own his internal process.] I no longer need to fear being lost or swallowed up by my subconscious energy.

From this vantage point, I also came to see that my introjects do not belong to my parents. It is true that others contributed to their formation, but they are in my consciousness so they are my responsibility. It was empowering to see that these introjects belong to me! They had seemed to possess me, but in fact, they were mine. I possessed them. And I was taking full responsibility for them. I would no longer be a victim. It was now up to me to let them go.

Struck by this insight and from the pure space of loving awareness I inquired, "in this moment can I feel hatred deep in my body." Yes, it was there under the surface. I opened to that darkness to feel the hatred and the desire to destroy. I sensed what felt like a beast – a green monster in my left eye, down the left side of my torso and into my arm. I fully owned its' existence. How could I not, it was occurring inside me.

In the face of that hatred and from a place of deep compassion, acceptance and humility I spoke acknowledging my traits of violence, rape, destruction, annihilation, ridicule, and belittling which I projected onto myself and others (my parents, partners, God, etc.). I asked for forgiveness. I said "I love you" and "thank you".

While working through this process, I saw that this energy was in conflict only with itself. There was no one out there. A deep sense of surrender then occurred. In a moment of grace, all traces of that deep-seated hatred vanished and have never returned. I was filled with gratitude.

More than ever, I now see that I am responsible for absolutely everything in my life. Embracing this responsibility has freed my heart to love my parents and others much more fully. The energies of strength, will and power which had been co-mingled with my deep seated resentments are now free to move in and out of consciousness unencumbered.

In conclusion, my development as a human being has been a long journey that continues. Through the experiential nature of ISP, my sense of self grew. Blocked energies were freed and I began to re-inhabit my body, which lifted me out of depression. These were things that traditional talk therapy had not been able to provide for me.

In ISP Jerry provided his stable support as we explored together the depths of my being. This is something for which I am deeply thankful. Discovering my own nature as stable awareness has allowed me to continue my transformation, and to take full responsibility for my conscious transformation.

I am particularly thankful to Jerry for providing a safe environment from which these aspects of body/mind could be explored, free of shame.

CHAPTER 7

Treatment of the Phallic Hysteric

Etiology

The phallic stage lasts from 3 to 6 years of age. In the phallic stage the girl develops strong psychosexual love impulses towards her father. She is in conflict: she fears rejection by her mother because of her incestuous longings for her father. Freud referred to this triangle as the Oedipus Complex. It is her fear of her mother's rejection that is the impetus for her to resolve the Oedipus complex; and this is assisted by her realization that the consummation of her incestuous feelings towards her father will not occur. The daughter draws closer to her mother and internalizes her mother's morals and values, which make up the core of the daughter's Conscience and Super-Ego. Then the phallic stage ends with this resolution of the Oedipus Complex.

The responses of her father to her love impulses are crucial in determining whether the daughter resolves her Oedipus Complex.

The fathers of hysterical daughters often are also fixated on their own phallic stage. They harbor incestuous urges towards their daughters but they also have ambivalent feelings about these urges. Socially buttressed morals against incest are very powerful. This shared ambivalence towards each other is the basis of a bond between father and daughter. The father attempts to distance himself from his daughter by putting her down, especially regarding her femininity. The daughter feels crushed and narcissistically wounded.

As an adult, she is strongly drawn to men. She also has intense anger at her father. Her anger at her father is repressed and, therefore, unconscious. This results in her getting hurt easily and feeling much shame. As a grown-up woman she submits passively to men with the hope they will take care of her.

As a woman, her unresolved Oedipus Complex results in lovemaking where her male partner is a stand-in for her father, and this is unconscious. She substitutes sex for love. This dilutes the disloyalty to her special, internalized relationship with her father.

Hysteric Body Structure

The phallic is a rigid character. Many of her muscles are tense. They take the form of a mesh or a chain mail net. While the muscles are tense they are also flexible. Additionally, other muscles are armored.

Bottom Half of the Body

The pelvis is blocked at the top, the waist, and this somatic split supports the psychological separation of sex from love (or her heart from her pelvis).

She does excessive pelvic movement that is exaggerated hip swinging. This is a way of parading her sexuality. And her excessive use of make-up is also an attempt to get attention from men.

The front and back of her pelvis is armored, the former is her repressed love and the latter is her repressed anger, both developed in her early relationship with her father. Along with this, her adductors are also armored. Therefore, she gets limited pleasure from her sexual activity.

Her legs are armored, so she is not well grounded.

Upper Half of the Body

This part of her body is deadened. The neck and jaw are armored. The muscles of the face are tight, so the hysteric looks younger than she actually is. As treatment proceeds, her face muscles relax and she increasingly wrinkles and looks older and more her actual age.

Her block at the waist limits her discharging of energy. (Discharge occurs as energy moves down from the head end into the pelvis.) This creates an emotional flatness. As energy builds up, this increases the likelihood of episodes of diffuse emotional flare-ups (this is the *hysteria*).

The Treatment of the Hysteric

The Use of Exercises

Exercises are used to increase grounding (e.g. the Side-to-Side movement and stress position). Then we use the backward bow and the forward arch to both increase grounding and to increase her energy level. This increase of energy fosters the increasing consciousness of her underlying feelings and needs. This initiates the process of de-armoring.

We also foster the enlivening of the lower half of the patient's body by using the Spread Eagle stress position. The position opens up the armored pelvis and adductors. And this stress position leads her to become more aware of her unconscious needs and feelings. She is able to work her feelings and fantasies with her father introject. Over time, this position and her elicited work help to deepen her sexual pleasure and to discharge her energy more fully (as energy moves from her head down to her pelvis). This mobilization reduces both the patient's level of anxiety and the diffuse, hysterical discharges of energy. This structural change is not sufficient unless the patient becomes aware of, and acts on her feelings towards her father introject.

The father's presence is invoked on a vertical mattress before the patient. She proceeds to talk and express first her anger at her father introject. When her feelings of anger are much reduced, she moves to expressing her love for him spontaneously. Then she is helped to cognitively integrate what he did to her and what she has expressed to him now. This is likely to include expressing her pent-up feelings towards him on the vertical mattress and then doing things to him now that she couldn't do to him then, such as expressing her anger at him. This finishing of the childhood trauma is crucial for the healing of the patient.

The Use of Touch Work

Generally, we work in the developmental sequence: head to tail. Therefore, work is initiated by using deep touch on her neck and shoulders. I work the muscles at the base of her skull and then the shoulder muscles. (Supervised training fosters doing this touch work effectively.) After a sequence of deep touch work, and the emotional work that is stimulated is fully expressed in sessions, we give soft, nurturing touch to these same muscles. Time is allowed for her to express the feelings elicited by soft touch. This deepens the process of de-armoring initiated by the exercises above. Generally, we sequence exercises and stress work first, followed by touch work.

She opens her throat by using the gag reflex. She places her index finger down her throat to the point that her gag reflex starts. Then she withdraws her finger short of vomiting. Unconscious feelings may emerge and she may be much more vocally responsive during subsequent touch work. Often her voice generally seems more open and expressive. Her subsequent work deepens from the opening of her throat.

Then comes hard touch work on the long muscles of the back as the patient lies in a prone position (see Illustration 4,). Recovery of traumatic memories and intense emotional work with her father introject often occurs. Likely, she expresses intense anger. Movement may then occur because of these touches. Eliciting her emotions, with her awareness of these feelings and with her movement/actions, helps her to integrate herself and to promote the development of her ego.

The therapist helps her to roll over on her back so that she is freer to move. Before she is completely finished emoting, work is done with her eyes as I described in the treatment of the schizoid (Illustration 8). This is the bringing of her feelings into her eyes. This eye work helps to de-armor her eye muscles and to integrate her head with her neck and body. After this work ends, soft touch is applied to her back muscles, those that received deep pressure.

Sequentially, then we do hard touch on the width of the pelvic hinge to loosen up the armoring of her waist.

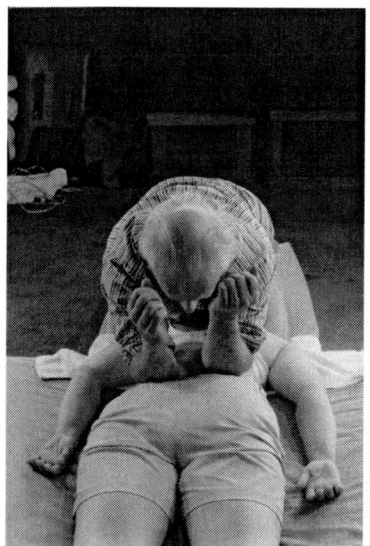

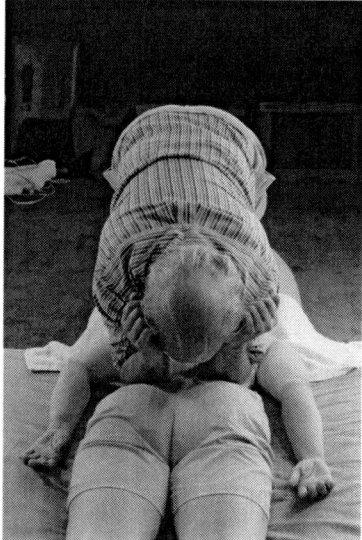

Greasing the Pelvic Hinge

Illustration 10. Greasing the Pelvic Hinge

The patient lies down in a prone position. Her therapist sits on his haunches on a pillow at the top of the mattress. The therapist starts the touch by placing his elbows on the hinge close to the spine and making sure not to press on it. He asks his patient to breathe deeply. Then he moves his weight over his elbows to deliver a hard catalytic touch to the hinge. He repeats this touch at least two more times to cover the width of her hinge. Then she expresses her feelings fully with the support of her therapist.

This reduces her top and bottom split. This fosters the integration of her heart and her sexuality. This also fosters her being more aware of her feelings and expressing them more fully, as her energy moves from her head end down towards her tail.

After she expresses what emerges for her, we use soft touch to her pelvic hinge.

Jerry Perlmutter, PhD

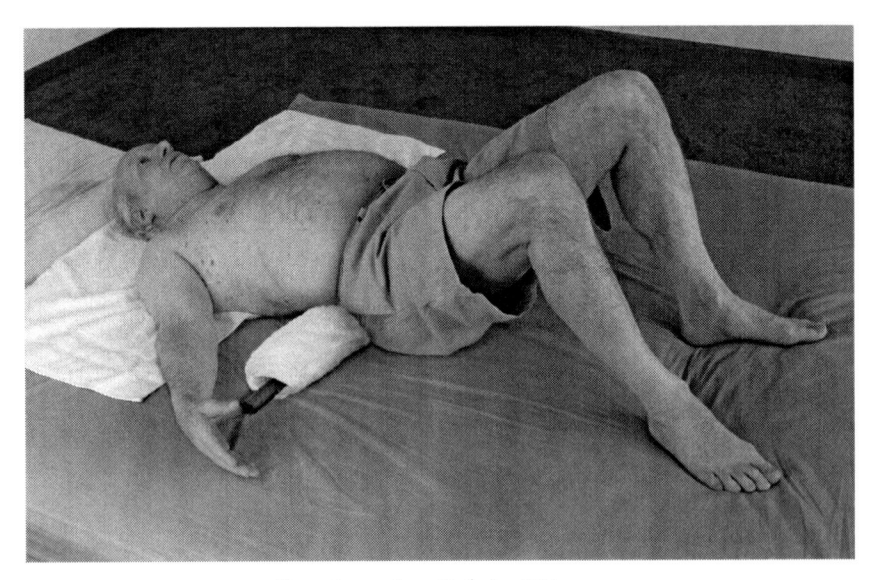

Resting the Pelvic Hinge

Illustration 11. Resting the Pelvic Hinge

The patient lies down in the supine position, with a roll placed under the width of her pelvic hinge. Then the therapist may use his open hands to touch the patient's pelvic hinge softly as she lies down in a prone position. Usually these soft touches work to help the patient to explore her feelings of love and sadness.

With the patient on her back, the therapist does hard touch to her abdominal muscles. Soft touch to these muscles follows this up. Then the therapist works the abductors and adductors of her thighs by using his thumbs on these muscles as the patient lies on her side with the bottom leg bent and up and forward so that he has access to both of her legs. Then she turns on her other side and he repeats these touches to the other adductor and abductor.

This touch work to her back, her pelvic hinge and her abductors and adductors is repeated till the patient expresses her damned up feelings fully. The therapist works with her until she completes her traumas. He can feel the muscles that he has worked. If these muscles have become soft, this corroborates that she has finished her back work and her work with her adductors and abductors. This is a large amount of intense touch work.

Again, each time she is triggered by exercises, or movement, or soft and hard touch, she expresses her feelings. When she works the trauma and the conflict with her father, she talks to "him" on the mattress. She is invited to also touch him and to move as she experiences and expresses emotions. This helps her to externalize her father introject and to redo and complete her earlier trauma. This process helps the hysteric to heal. This type of healing process applies to the treatment of all of the character types.

Dealing with her love and anger towards her father helps her to separate herself from him. And this provides her with an opportunity to finally resolve her Oedipus Complex. She identifies with her mother and internalizes her morals and values. This resolution also opens her up to having fuller relationships with men that include the melding of love and sex.

Reducing her armoring at her pelvic hinge reduces the split between her upper and lower body. Energy can flow more fully from her head to her pelvis. This flow of energy helps her to discharge her energy and thereby to get fuller and deeper sexual satisfaction. There is no damming up of her energy, so that she no longer has hysterical outbursts. Generally, she can lead a more integrated life.

I am sorry that I have no patient narrative for the Phallic Hysterical character. I have never had one in my practice, nor have any of my colleagues had one. We are all males and this is a factor. I do not wish to speculate any further about why this is so.

CHAPTER 8

The Treatment of the Phallic Narcissist

Etiology

During the Phallic Stage (3-6 years) the mother, and father are very demanding of their child. They pressure the child to be a certain way that meets their unmet needs. Their hope is that their child will complete them, and their stake in this happening is very great. This is a parental prescription for their child's *false self*. The development of a false self may actually be more complicated because the son probably develops false selves in service to the different needs of his mother and father.

In the oral stage, the narcissistic child does not go through the normal task of ego development where his ego would naturally be deflated. He doesn't go through this normal struggle where the child tries to fend off the parent's setting of limits, like the mother leaving him for a while. Yet, she does this separation with empathy for her child's discomfort with the separation when she returns. She meets his feelings of separation anxiety with her expressions of her love for him. As the mother leaves,

Healing Body, Self and Soul

gradually the child is able to internalize her soothing and move towards separating psychologically from her. As a result, he realizes that he is not in charge and he is not omnipotent. Normally, losing these battles in a loving relationship helps the child leave behind grandiosity.

For the narcissistic child, the parents are very much invested in getting the child to accept them leaving in a much more coercive manner. The child does not have the opportunity to feel soothed and loved by his mother as she begins to separate from him. Therefore, he continues to feel grandiose as he develops past the oral stage and eventually into the phallic stage.

The relationship between the narcissistic child and his parent(s) is complex. The child follows the prescribed false self lest the mother and father disapprove of him and they withdraw their acceptance, and they may punish him severely (for example, by beating him) for not living up to the behavior the parent needs from him. His parents exert much power in the relationships with their child. The child also has power because the parents need him to conform to their prescriptions for him so that they feel completed; the parents are also dependent on their child. The child's power reinforces his grandiosity; he feels in charge too. Much of the dynamics between the son and his parents is below the level of awareness. This hampers them from taking steps that would resolve these issues.

As an adult, the narcissist lives in fear that he is not good enough to get his father's approval. The demanding phallic father is the source of standards for the boy as he traverses the phallic stage. Thus the boy is driven to perform at a very high level. He competes intensely with others. He tries to look very competent, yet he is driven by fear of disapproval. So this drive is compensatory, which makes the narcissistic shakier than he shows to others. He also has repressed anger at the parent(s) who coerced him. This anger also fuels his competitiveness. Fear and anger leads him to show great persistence in his achievements,

109

and this is a reflection of his tendency to hold on to tasks. The narcissistic exhibits potency, in the sense of having many sexual experiences, yet he gets little pleasure from each one. When he can't alter his low level of pleasure, he seeks other women to have sex with hoping that he will get more satisfaction with new partners. This does not work for him. The sources of this shortcoming come from within himself.

The Freudian view has the trauma in the narcissist's phallic phase being very intense, which leads to the son's fixation on this phase. The lack of resolution of separation from his parents in the oral phase indicates the child is also fixated on the oral stage. The child feels a threat of castration by the father for the child's genital activities and fantasies. For the narcissism to occur, the father's threat to the child is great because of the father's intense investment in his child's behavior, as described above. The father supports the mother's severe discipline. At the same time, the child also fears the mother's disapproval and the loss of her love. The narcissist's mother is much more severe than many other mothers. She has an extreme need for her son to act in ways that complete her. This leads the child to have intense, traumatic experiences connected to the Oedipus Complex, and these traumas undermine its resolution.

Phallic-Narcissistic Body Structure

The body is very athletic-looking in that his muscles are well developed and well toned. He has wide shoulders, a broad chest and a narrow waist. The broad shoulders are the result of the child having to take responsibility (for his parent's well-being) early in his life. The broad chest is the result of the narcissist's breathing being frozen as his chest is locked in inspiration. This is how he defends against feeling and expressing soft feelings of sorrow and how he protects his heart from being intensely hurt. Breathing is primarily abdominal. His shoulder girdle is tight. The diaphragm is locked in a descended position.

His eyes are lively and expressive. The mouth is softer. The jaw is set and determined--to be successful by trying hard. The throat is constricted to hold in his voice from expressing feelings of sadness and anger directed at his parents.

This character's body is enclosed in a wire mesh, thus we call the narcissist a rigid character. This mesh enclosure helps this person to resist the tremendous pressure he is under to perform in order to satisfy both of his parents. The mesh narrows and reduces the movement of energy towards the tail, the genital. This underlies the lack of satisfaction from sexual intercourse because the energy cannot move easily to the tail, so sexual discharges are limited in intensity. This sexuality of the person impels him to persist by doing multiple, serial, sexual acts in an attempt to get satisfaction. *Again, he does not face that he is the source of his limited sexual gratification.*

The phallic's mesh leads this character to be referred to as a *rigid character*. The extensive mesh results in this person's body being numb. The narcissist is not aware of his numbness. All characters have some numbness in their body due to their armoring, but the narcissist's numbing is much more extensive and intensive than the other character types.

The narcissist is armored at the waist or the pelvic hinge, which also hampers the movement of energy to the genital area. This also impedes the discharge of sexual energy and other types of energy, e.g., work, play and creative energy. The narcissist has a high level of energy, but it serves the false self, which hampers him in utilizing his energy fully. *Literally, his heart is not in his strivings.* His energy does not connect with the energy resources of his self, since the false self shrouds the self.

The legs are an extension of the pelvis; they are armored, too. Grounding is an issue.

Jerry Perlmutter, PhD

The Therapy of the Narcissist

It is important for the therapist to provide a safe, protective and supportive setting for her patient. This in itself is emotionally corrective or healing for the patient. He lacked this during his childhood. In therapy, he is no longer being pushed to be a certain way. Actually, the therapist helps him to get in touch with his authentic self; she is accepting of whatever emerges from his depths and supports him in expressing himself more fully. These are all intense healing factors.

The therapist asks her patient to do the backward bow and forward arch to increase his grounding, and to stimulate an even greater build up of energy, and subsequently a fuller discharge of energy and feelings. This work immediately addresses the narcissist's pathological energy cycle: lots of energy that dribbles out very little at a time, so there is not much release, relief and gratification. The stress work requires the patient to stretch and compress a large number of muscles in his body, and this in itself reduces armoring throughout the body. The stress work generally reduces the tightness and numbness of his body; this also supports his fuller energy release.

Next, the therapist loosens up the constriction of his jaw, neck and throat: this is referred to as the oral ring. She does this by applying hard touch to these muscles, followed by soft touch. The neck is the narrowest part of the body. Therefore, it is a most effective place to constrict the flow of energy between the head and the body. This touch work opens up an important path for the patient's release. Previously, with the hysteric, you were told about having the patient elicit their gag reflex as a way of opening the armored throat. This intervention applies to the narcissistic character too.

The next site to work is the top of the patient's shoulders. Taking on the false self is quite a burden, and he bears the burden in his armored shoulders. Applying deep touch and then soft touch does this de-armoring.

Healing Body, Self and Soul

Then the chest is worked (see Illustration 6,). This is how a sequence of interventions is formulated and implemented. The chest is pressed to soften the chest and to lengthen the exhalation. The patient lies down on the mattress in a supine position. The therapist kneels on a pillow, behind her patient's head. She places her hands (palm down) on his chest. Her fingers are extended and close to each other. The fingertips of her two hands touch each other. (If the patient is female the therapist avoids contact with her nipples so she does not sexually stimulate her.) The therapist breathes with her patient. Upon exhale, the therapist comes up on her knees, lengthen her arms and puts the weight of her body over her hands. She applies this pressure a little longer than her patient's exhale. This lengthens and deepens the patient's exhale. Again, as the therapist does this, she notices the flexibility of the patient's chest to gauge how much pressure to apply to do the two subsequent touches on exhalation. After the three touches, the therapist breaks contact with the patient.

Often the patient will respond to these touches with an outburst of emotion and action. This reaction is possible because of the de-armoring done so far in the therapy. This increased awareness of feelings undermines the repression required to live out of the false self. The patient may get angry and yell at his mother to stop pressuring him. The therapist intervenes to intensify the patient's experience: she says loudly, "Tell your mother to stop pressuring you, again!"

After this intense outbreak is completed, the patient may then remember a specific experience of being pressured during his childhood. He may deeply experience his anger for the first time. In childhood, he was unable to resist. The patient is able to express intense feeling, to let himself know more fully what was at stake for him then. If the patient chooses to beat on the mattress as he talks to his mother, he allows himself to act now in ways he couldn't let himself do then as a child. So the patient regresses back to his childhood at a time he experienced trauma. He goes through the experience, letting himself complete his trauma. This deep touch work to the chest may last several sessions, until the armoring is softened and his breathing is much deeper and fuller, especially his exhale.

We then move to open up his breathing more by working to loosen his diaphragm.

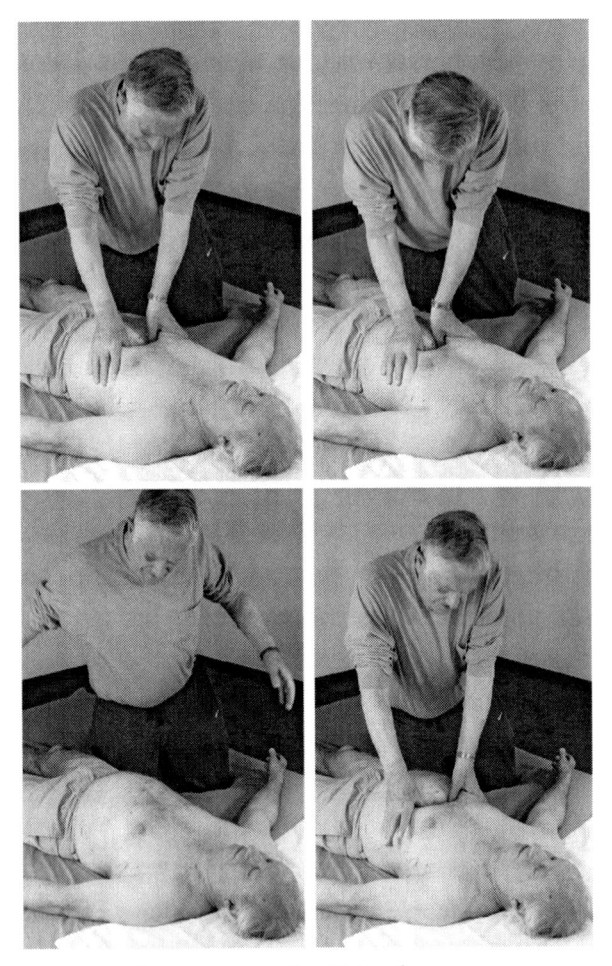

Loosening the Diaphragm

Illustration 12. Loosening the Diaphragm

Healing Body, Self and Soul

We continue the breath work with this touch. Here we use hard, deep touch on the diaphragm to further open up the patient's breathing. The illustration shows the position of the therapist as she administers the first of the three touches to the diaphragm. The patient lies down in the supine position. The therapist sits on her haunches to the left of the patient's right hip. She faces her patient. She leans over to her right so that her hands reach both sides of the patient's diaphragm. The therapist starts this touch at the middle of his diaphragm, with each thumb avoiding touching the middle of the abdomen, which is calcified and readily identified. She asks her patient to breathe deeply and she breathes with him. As he finishes an inhale, she comes up on her knees and pushes her thumbs into his abdomen and then up towards the diaphragm.

This can be a very painful touch initially, especially if the diaphragm is very tight. She gives the patient some time to recover. Then she repeats this touch two more times coming out wider so the second touch is about half way from the center of the diaphragm to the outside of the diaphragm where the ribs come down. The third touch is at the place where the ribs come down almost at his sides. Touches two and three are also done as the patient finishes inhaling. This sequence of touches must be done repeatedly before the diaphragm loosens up and the pain dissipates. These loosening touches foster the descending of the diaphragm and the deepening of his exhalation, and then his inhalation.

Soft touch to the chest starts when there is time to do it after the deep touch work is completed during a session. Soft touch is done with the therapist laying along side her patient on her right side. She can use the touch we described earlier (Illustration 7,), Holding His Heart Between Her Hands, as she breathes with her patient. This is an intense touch. This touch may elicit sadness because *he didn't feel loved for who he was* by his mother. As he says this to his elicited image of his mother on a mattress before him, the therapist says,

Notice if your arms want to move. He stretches his arms towards the presence of his mother and continues talking to her. The therapist supports a deeper emotional expression of his sadness.

This soft work also is repeated several times until his sadness is reduced and the re-experiencing of being unloved leads to a completion of this memory and a resolution of this trauma. He often gets to the place where he reaches to his mother on the mattress, touches her softly, telling her that he loves her. Though forgiving his mother is difficult because his mother pressured him so much and so broadly.

Next in the sequence of work is loosening the pelvic hinge. This is accomplished by doing deep touch work on the full width of the hinge as the patient lies down in a prone position. Then the therapist does soft touch to the hinge. The therapist uses her hands to do soft touch to the width of the hinge.

Next the adductors and abductors of the thighs are worked. Whenever possible we work on the two sets of muscles that are in opposition to each other. We do deep touch work on these muscles going sequentially up the muscles towards his pelvis. The patient lies on his side with the leg bent as it is being worked on the bottom, as the other leg lies straight.

After the touch work we often do structured exercises on these two sets of muscles. The patient lies down in a supine position. He raises his knees up so that his feet are flat on the mattress. He places his legs almost together. The therapist stands with legs spread apart on the sides of her patient's legs. The patient is told to exert maximum effort to spread the therapist's legs apart. After resting, the therapist goes on to stand between the patient's legs spread about 18 inches apart. Now the patient is asked to exert maximum effort to push the therapist's legs together. This successive work reduces the armoring

Healing Body, Self and Soul

in the abductors and adductors. Elicited feelings are allowed their fullest expression.

The last touch should be soft, to follow the above catalytic touches, by having the patient lie on his side with the leg under him bent. Then the therapist uses soft touch along the adductors. This is repeated on the other leg. Then the patient continues lying on his side with both legs bent slightly. The therapist applies soft touch to the patient's thigh. Then the patient lays on his other side and soft touch is applied to the other thigh. Again, elicited feelings are allowed their fullest expression.

A soft touch that supports the patient while he encounters his parent(s) is very effective at this stage of the work. This is the Easy Chair.

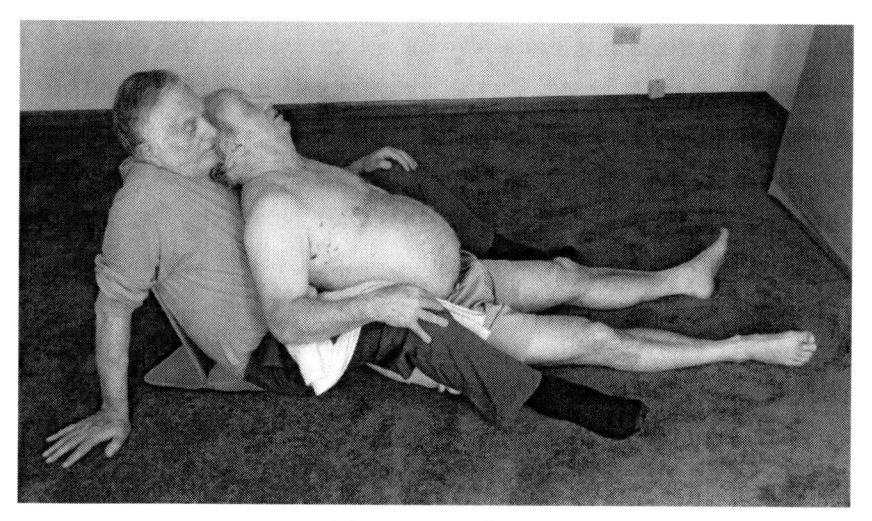

The Easy Chair

Illustration 13. The Easy Chair

Likely, this is an intense soft touch. (Notice the importance of this touch in the narration by the patient at the end of this chapter.) The therapist uses support for her back as she sits down and extends her legs forward. She places a large bath towel over her genital area to avert sexually stimulating herself and her patient. The patient sits down between her legs and leans back. He places his arms over her her knees. Usually a mattress is placed up against the wall in front of the patient before they sit down. If it fits, he can see his mother or father on the mattress facing him, he can talk to the parent, and he can get up and touch the parent via touching the mattress. He has the benefit of a very supportive touch from his therapist as he does this. This is a process that helps the patient to melt the mold that his parents have held him in, the false self. The patient experiences the height of the externalization of his parental introjects.

A Summary of the Strategy of Healing the Phallic Narcissist

All of the interventions above play the important function of reducing and removing the false self. We then help the patient to restore and bring to consciousness his inner, authentic feelings. The stress work operates to undermine the numbness throughout his body by focusing on his core and his arms and legs. Deepening his breathing also supports his becoming more alive and having more intense experiences and discharges of his feelings. And working his large muscles also reduces his numbing of his authentic self. Along with this muscle work, the patient accesses traumatic memories with his parents in his childhood. By completing these memories, he heals his trauma.

This ends the presentation of intervention sequences for the Narcissistic patient using the framework of the Reichian body types.

A Phallic Narcissistic Patient's Testimony

[What change did you want from your therapy at the beginning? Did you achieve this change? Describe the course of this change over time. If you have knowledge of how your therapy helped you to achieve this, please describe it.]

I started therapy because my wife recommended it as part of our separation. I knew my life had been unsatisfying, but I had no idea why, nor did I know how to change myself or in what direction to even go. [Here he tells how much his false self took over his life without his awareness.] The process of discovering how I had been abused, how I felt abandoned even as a child, how demanding my mother had been all my life, and how much influence she (and later my wife) had exerted on my life was extraordinary. I discovered how interconnected my feelings (or lack thereof) and my body rigidness and numbness were. As I gained feeling in my body, I also gained an awareness of my emotions and how they had been held in check for so many years. [Here is a person who gets in touch with how much his life did not reflect who he was; he was not aware of this! He was not conscious of how much his mother determined who he could be. This is the central situation of the Phallic Narcissist.]

Through touch therapy I began to experience my body —it's pains, it's desires—and by getting in touch with my body, I began to get in touch with my emotions— fear of abandonment, fear of true success, anger with the authority figures in my life, frustration at my lack of ability to choose my own path. I had turned my life over to other people in my life, and through therapy, I was able to recover much of my own power—power to make my own choices, to resist the manipulations of others, to try new ways of doing myself. Of course, these discoveries and the resultant changes in my life took place over the course of more than six years. However, the knowledge that I could change and the awareness that my body had become numb and my emotions were pushed down to the point of non- existence were seen very early in my therapy.

[Your mother was intense with you about your getting good grades. This was important to her because she didn't see herself as bright. What did she do to push you to get good grades?] My mother shamed my brother and me when we didn't meet her expectations— not that we weren't good enough. I didn't live up to her expectations of me. You dummied yourself down— that was her attitude, her demeaning tone of voice. She did that to me in front of my brother, in front of my dad. It didn't make any difference who was there.

Even at her late age today she still has the same qualities. She still hits me. This was her form of discipline. She sent me to my room, but that was after a paddling. She used a paddle. She took off the string and the ball. The paddle was ½ inch thick. It wasn't enough to leave marks, but it stung and hurt. That was her intent, to hurt. She is still the same way. She punches me in the arm. She punches me on the back. She still lashes out. She hasn't changed in all these years. She goes back and forth a lot now. [What do you mean?] I'm a loving son. She has dementia; she doesn't remember 10 minutes ago. If I am there, I am still her loving son, except if I cross her in any way—it's a punch, or you are a bad boy. It's the same quality of life, the same attitude.

[What was your relationship with your father?] He was never the disciplinarian. I think this is true with many fathers, living out their fantasies through their sons. The only sport he was allowed to play was baseball. He lived through us in sports: baseball, basketball, football and tennis. It was there that he pushed us. I still remember when I was ten. I was in a Little League. At ten I was B level. That was where I was supposed to be. But they needed a catcher at A level. Dad volunteered me—he pushed me. I was catching boys who were two years older than me and thirty pounds heavier. That first summer I spent with my left hand bruised. It never went away. In football he pushed us to play. Our coach was the same way. They'd say if it rains or is cold, it doesn't matter. You are football players, and you go out and you play. I played an entire game in sleet, and I was eleven years old. He was like that in every sport. He was always pushing us to be the best players. He and I pushed me into the All-Star team in Little League. I took a year off in the Pony League. He told one of the coaches who needed a catcher that I was good and available.

I enjoyed sports, but it was with a high cost. And I am still that way with myself. When I was 35 my kids were in gymnastics. I used to help out a little bit. I was invited by one of the gymnastic coaches to try one of the sets my kids were learning. Oh yeah—I hurt myself in my wrists. I ended up with tendonitis, with a detached retina. I ended up with a lot of injuries. You don't start gymnastics at 35—well the sane man doesn't do it. But there is insanity about that quality of pushing myself.

[Did you take in your father's pressuring you?] Yes, he said you play through injuries. At one point in the Pony League, I slid into third base. I got a hairline fracture in my foot. I was back playing in the next game. I never missed a game or a time at bat. [Did your father push you to do that?] It was a part of life. It's not broken. That's the way life was for him. He was never a disciplinarian. I never remember him hitting me. It was to get out there and play. [His father's prescription for him is different than his mother's prescription. He had to play at a high level of performance and to do this even when conditions hampered him from doing so.]

In the last two weeks I read my early journals of therapy. What I found out is that I forgot it; I put it out of my mind, how much hurt I relived in those early sessions. I relived my hurt not only from my parents, but also from going through the early stages of separation and divorce.

Remembering from the journal was like remembering a bad dream. I worked my way through it. I am very studied about whom I now have relationships with. I move on if a relationship is not productive with a person.

I was thinking about this. Can I read it to you from my journal 4 months into therapy? Life is and continues to be unfair. My wife lays down rules and I am expected to live by these rules. And when I lived by the rules the authorities changed the rules often without telling me. I got caught from expecting praise for following the rules. I got reprimanded for not following the rules. My parents kept raising the bar. I couldn't meet their expectations. Every time I came close they raised the bar. [He fuses his parents with his former wife; he has strong transference feelings from his mother to his wife.]

I still need the caresses of a mother. Just to be held by my mother close to her breast, with her heart matching mine. She didn't want to reveal her secret self. I didn't want to reveal how needy I was. I wanted to be caressed without reservation. How unloved and hurt I felt. I amaze myself with how my body continues to soften— not that I have less power. I am stronger than I was in those days. I have feelings everywhere. When I get a massage these days, it is like heaven, pure joy.

My wife never let go of my history [his sexual affairs]. Before we got divorced, her remarks were made to me directly. After our divorce her comments became more tangential. [He laughs as he sees the parallels between his mother and wife.]

[I want to review with you some of your sexual history. You have a history of having sexual affairs with women, lots of them, right?] Yes, we got married early in my military service. So I had affairs then, and also when we came back to civilian life. My sexual history went back to when I was fifteen. And I was always active. The thing was, after I got married, a lot of it had to do with times I felt abandoned by my wife for one reason or another.

When we came home from the Army, she went back to school to finish up her Bachelor's degree. She was busy day and night. If she wasn't studying and doing homework, she was busy working. She didn't have time for me. And then she became involved in church. I wasn't involved in church for a couple of years. She used to go to church meetings with her mother during the week. When I came home from work, I got our children. I got to do the grocery shopping. And I got to do everything with them. I made supper. And I got to carry them wherever they needed to go. I'd get up four to five in the morning to go to work. She slept in. I would go to sleep at ten in the evening. And she worked 35 hours a week. For evenings and Saturday the kids were mine while she worked and then went to church in the evenings. So she had less and less time for me.

Then for ten or twelve years, we did have church work together. So we spent the most time together in my marriage. My sexual liaisons stopped. I was faithful to her during the last twenty years of our relationship. That was the best years of our marriage for me.

[Was the twelve-step program you participated in useful to you?] It got me out of porn. When my wife and I had sex, I was into porn. I remember seeing it in my head. I wasn't truly with her all of the time. I was into my own fantasy. [So he "abandoned" his wife too.]

[Did the character of your sexual experiences change after being in ISP therapy?] I haven't had much experience since therapy. I had sex a few times with a woman I dated. My fiancée and I have never been to bed together. This was a point of agreement between us—that we would wait until we got married. I don't have enough data to answer that question. I haven't had any sex with anyone for six or seven years. [This ceasing of being sexual, of controlling his sexuality by mutual agreement with his fiancé, talks to his shift from being freely sexual with many partners. For him this is an indication of his healing.]

[Is there anything else you want to tell me from your researching your therapy journals?] There was one thing that had to do with emotions. Neither one of my parents would allow us to cry. When we were being punished and cried they said don't cry, you're a boy—a man from a very young age. Yes, that was our German heritage. I am totally German, absolute discipline. We were Catholic German—very rigid. My grandma was very rigid. You only played with the good kids, not the bad kids. If the kids did anything wrong, they were bad. There wasn't a good thing about them. If I did something wrong, you need to correct it.

When I went back to my house [these days] because of its' flooding, I looked over what my mother gave to me. She had my grade cards all the way back to my first grade. I went through them. And there was only one mark that was bad on each card. If I had straight A's in my classes, it was my conduct that was blemished. There was always a blemish on my report card. I couldn't or wouldn't fulfill her need to have a perfect little boy. [Here is another phallic narcissistic dynamic. While his mother used her power to shape him, he also did some controlling of his mother.]

I obviously made my mother suffer. I never had a perfect report card.

I think the big disappointment was the time I chose to get married in a Protestant church. I chose to marry a Protestant girl. And to this day, even in her dementia, this rankles her that I am not Catholic anymore. But I am not sure when I stopped caring about it, certainly before I got married. I stopped caring about what she felt anymore because I was numb to her. I just disconnected from her.

When I revisit my marriage, I see where I married my mother. I married someone who would direct my life for me. For many years Mom set down the rules. I couldn't live by them. My wife also set down the rules. [Give some examples.] We were going to go to church. She told me what kind of house we were going to have, and the kinds of friends we were going to have. She was going back to school to get her Master's and Doctorate degrees. I said, "Yeah, I could live with all that". I couldn't live with all that, obviously. I'd always act out. But it was easier for me to disconnect, the same way I disconnected from my Mom. And I don't want to do all of that anymore. [His self-disconnection helped him to act out of his false self.]

My current fiancée and I have arguments. She is not accustomed to that with her first two husbands. Now she has someone who wants to make decisions with her. It has been good for both of us because we have a give and take; we learn about each other. We have so many things in common. Some things we are at opposite ends of the spectrum.

I love to play golf. If I made a bad shot, I'd swear. I could not accept myself making bad shots. Now, I don't throw clubs; I don't swear. I don't need to do that anymore. I do feel that twinge now. I still have this drive for perfection, and that I have struggled with all of my life. I am working on accepting less than the best from me.

We have talked about my abandonment issues. I always enjoyed sex all those years. It didn't matter whom I was with. I think part of it is the intimacy of it—which I lacked for so many years. I had sex to compensate by being intimate, whether it was with my wife or the girl next door. It was a striving for mutual fulfillment—two people coming together.

When I was working on myself, I learned more about the pain in my back, at my waist [his pelvic hinge] in my conforming to expectations, both other's and mine. I could feel the push in my lower back—go do your homework, go study—win. It was the same push to go out and beat someone. Their expectations would become my expectations. I would feel guilt when I let them down. I was a failure. I was learning how to heal myself—how to forgive myself and how to put myself back together.

[Say more about forgiving yourself.] I still screw up; make mistakes. I am better at forgiving myself. It takes me a while. Instead of beating myself up for having missed the mark again, being able to stop and talk down my anxiety, to let me be less than perfect, and to accept this as being the best I can do in the moment. And this has a transforming effect of my attitude toward myself.

[In ISP did you have experiences that were spiritual?] When I was growing up I don't remember times when my parents were physically loving to me—cuddling, holding, touching softly. Yet the experience that had the most profound impact on my life prior to therapy was a preaching I heard at a Christian camp. The minister was preaching on the Love of the Father. He said that God, unlike our human fathers, loved us perfectly, that He wanted us to crawl up into His lap, lay our head on His shoulder, lean into His chest and feel His arms wrap around us, protecting and comforting us like no other person could. This was my <u>one</u> experience of this kind of love and care until my therapist sat on the floor and invited me to sit between his legs and just be held by him—just as I pictured my heavenly Father doing for me. [See Illustration 13, The Easy Chair.] This action for me was the real connection of the *human and the divine*.

How has your life changed because of your therapy?] My life is significantly different. I have explored avenues I hadn't dreamed of—travel, new people and a new profession though it is now only part-time. I make my own decisions and have confidence that the decisions I make are right for me. I have learned to live with disappointment—in people and circumstances. I have learned to say NO and to pick and choose what I want to be involved in.

Having tried talk therapy on two previous occasions to no avail, I found ISP a refreshing change that helped me to explore myself, to reclaim much "lost" experience that, once reclaimed, helped me to build a new life. Today I experience my emotions without the fear of losing myself in them. Joy, sorrow, love, anger, and peace—all are fully available to me and I rejoice in them.

Wrapping up Character and Body Therapy

Patients Primarily Determine When to Terminate ISP

The therapy work presented here usually takes years to do because the active interventions of ISP spawns a multitude of experiences that are important in healing the character shaping trauma of childhood. Patients choose to end therapy at different times in the therapy. Some persons choose to leave when their psychological and body symptoms are worked through. Others choose to stay to do deep soul work. Endings are made at all points between these extremes. Ultimately, the choice of when to terminate is heavily determined by the patient.

Early in my work, I had a patient who was in her late thirties. She used her therapy sessions very effectively. Her symptoms were abating and her energy was increasing. Suddenly she announced in therapy that she was quitting her treatment. She had finally met a man who was interested in her amorously, and they were talking about marrying. She developed a belief that this type of body therapy, if it was carried on further, would lead her to become "elite". She was concerned that this would separate her from her boyfriend (she implied that he was average). She was clear and certain about her decision.

This experience started me on the path to seeing the patient primarily making the decision about when to terminate therapy. And in doing so, we once again exclaim that this is the patient's therapy; that the therapist is there to help, and not to own nor determine the course of work. Admittedly, there are patients whose degrees of psychopathology are major, and they need unusual degrees of help and structuring until their treatment provides them with sufficient healing so that they are able to proceed with the usual degree of self-determination that a patient in ISP has.

ISP and the Process of Transformative Change

I am using the term transformation for a dramatic change in a person's form (body) or psychological essence. This change results in a vast improvement of the person. It is the therapist's use of process interventions (rather than suggesting content that the patient should "work") that supports the occurrence of transformative change. The patient determines the work agenda through what emerges in their experience. The therapist supports the fuller exploration of his thoughts, feelings and action. The ensuing paradoxical change occurs spontaneously. The specific changes emerge from the patient. Calling these changes improvements is based upon the patient's valuing of his changes.

Actually, there are a multitude of factors that initiate transformative change. And I will summarize them to make them explicit and clearer to the reader.

The therapy workroom is sound insulated so that patients feel free to express any feeling and action that emerges in them during a session. The room's floor and its' contents are padded so that patients are not concerned about being injured and are enabled to be spontaneous.

Early in sessions patients are asked to do stress work so that experiences that are close to being conscious emerge into a patient's awareness. And these exercises also increase groundedness so that the patient is supported from within to express himself spontaneously. ISP therapists introduce processes that help patients to explore these experiences more fully. For example, deep touch readily elicits regression to early trauma, which provides opportunities to relive and work them.

Many of the experiences that surface are unfinished trauma from early childhood. Trauma has this tendency to surface again and again until they are finished. This is a *species* process that supports healing. We have patients evoke the presence of their parents, often on mattresses opposite them. This set-up promotes the expression of many different feelings and a variety of different types of action, with a high degree of safety for the patient. This helps patients to externalize their introjects, which is an important aspect of healing.

If the patient persists in this reliving of trauma until they are finished, they experience the paradox of change, which insures that they can explore different facets of their early relationships so they complete their trauma and heal. After patients complete their trauma, they move on to Stage 2 of ISP. Here they explore their Self and Soul.

Not all patients experience transformational change. In this document, the phallic narcissist patient experiences coming alive emotionally that is gradual and ongoing throughout his therapy. Eventually, he made contact with his deep self so that he directs his own life in an authentic manner.

The masochistic patient gradually increased his awareness and expression of anger towards his mother for constantly punishing him. He detaches himself from his mother's criticism and increasingly feels better about himself.

All of the change of the patients is spontaneous and self-directed.

CHAPTER 9

Identifying More Healing Interventions Of Integrative Somatic Psychotherapy

Introduction

Many interventions are used to conduct ISP. Many have been already covered in this writing. There is not enough room and time to cover them all. There are still some important interventions to introduce you to here.

Concretizing Metaphors

When to use this intervention—Most often this intervention is used when a patient is stuck and unable to move to a more effective place. In this situation, the therapist is likely to introduce the intervention by developing and stating a metaphor. Less often, the patient initiates the intervention by spontaneously stating a metaphor during a session to communicate they are feeling stuck.

Healing Body, Self and Soul

Overall description of the intervention—The patient feels stuck and unable to break through. The therapist suggests a metaphor, attempting to use it to capture major qualities of the patient's situation. He tests the suitability of the metaphor with the patient. If it does not fit well for her, they work together to adapt it or come up with another metaphor, one that fits her situation better. Then he has the patient *act* on the metaphor so her situation is changed in a major way.

A more specific description of the intervention—Initially, the patient generates a description of her stuck situation. This description often consists of ideas and, at best, some feelings of frustration and irritability. For body psychotherapists, this description does not have a body basis, nor does it have actionable aspects that aid in breaking through her impasse. The patient's use of a metaphor yields more *tangible and elaborate meanings than the ideas* that the patient initially uses to capture her impasse. The patient acts on this metaphor and its many meanings. In doing so the patient dramatically alters her position in a direct manner that impels her breakthrough actions. She successfully moves herself through her impasse. Acting on a metaphor is a dramatic experience. It commands her attention. Her clear action helps her to fully perceive and own the changes she makes. This is an important therapeutic benefit. The therapist tests this by asking her how she feels after her action. He looks for feelings of relief and for other changes in her experience that indicate that she has broken through her impasse.

A Patient Narrative of Concretizing a Metaphor

> I remember that I'd worn a new white cotton dress to my body therapy session the day a particularly horrific [sexual] abuse memory surfaced in me. I felt my skin was smeared with bodily shame, my sense of self covered over in sticky, thick layers. With Jerry, I

moved through my memory of this experience until I could imagine wiping the residues of that trauma off me, and I began to feel new, changed, atoned and amazed—inside and out. [She generated the metaphor and the concretizing action: wiping off the residue of the trauma on herself.]

Then Jerry offered me the use of the shower in the bathroom in the session workroom. [I expanded on the concretizing of her metaphor after the formal session was over.] I could continue the cleaning process there on my own, he said, if I chose, before I left for the day. I accepted his offer as fitting. I was able to wash the coating of abuse and terror away twice, as if shedding skin I'd outgrown—once with movement during the session, once with soap and water and a thick towel in private, on my own. *It helped tremendously to know that I had the ability to clean up by myself.* I tear up, remembering this gift of grace even now [These last two sentences are an experience of gratitude as well as relief.] Sometimes when I feel covered by memory, I remember that session, and how it's possible for me to wash it away. [This is the relief that accompanies her breaking through her stuckness, to a way of transcending her abuse.]

Another Patient's Narrative of Concretizing a Metaphor

Growing up in a family in which my mother was an empty and orally needy human being, who actually had babies to suck the energy out of them in order to fill her endless internal abyss. It is utterly obvious that my own internal experience would be of being intensely "smothered." I was enmeshed into her neediness and unable neither to separate emotionally nor to individuate into some form of a psychologically independent being. With the only awareness that existed in my self was that "something is wrong with me" and when I was in interaction with my mother or other women, I experienced a continual low grade seething anger and frustration. Again, I was almost totally unaware of what this frustration and anger was about or of the origins of this slow burn.

So, I live a life. All I know is that all of my relationships with women leave me feeling clung to and engulfed, with the extreme need to escape and run away from this overwhelming wave of energy coming from each of the women I was involved with. Wondering, only slightly, how do I continue to get involved with the same type of needy and empty woman? What is my part in this? And why, no matter how hard I try to alter this pattern, it continues to happen in the same obnoxiously similar manner?

My desperation grows. Some resource in me moves me to seek some assistance. I know that I'm blind to what my contribution is to what is occurring. I have the wisdom to realize there is no way I am able to step outside of my self enough to understand and shift this relationship pattern.

So I begin psychotherapy. A major component is an intensive workshop involving body-centered psychotherapy [The Body, Self and Soul Workshop]. Participants select a new name for themselves in the weeklong experience, which serves to maintain my confidentiality and at the same time to name the emotional state I am in as I enter the workshop. Appropriately, I select the name "Rip Away".

During the workshop, I participate in an exercise that involves my making body contact with a mattress that is on its side and against a wall. Others slam the side of their body into the mattress. I end up lying down prone on the mattress falling into my internal experience as I described before. Once again I have that slow burn and the words spontaneously arise, "get the f* off of me." Before any realization occurs of what is happening, another mattress is thrust on me covering my back. An intense weight is applied to my back, which I soon realized was my therapist, providing exactly the experience I have lived with my entire life, only greatly exaggerated. Now, ultimately, I was being utterly and totally "SMOTHERED". My childhood and lifetime experience and the desperation in each and every relationship were being recreated in an utterly primal and concrete manner. This is my life; right now, right here. [The metaphor was suggested by my patient: his phrase, "get the f* off of me" so I get on a mattress that I put on his back.]

My slow burn instantly flamed into a rage. Lying there smothered, with apparently nothing else to do but tolerate it, I was in my own lifelong personal living hell. Until I hear the words, "Lay there and tolerate this or do something." [Says his therapist!] My rage explodes and I throw off the mattress [with his therapist] with an intense energy striving for space and freedom. I am free. And then the mattress is thrust back on me [along with his therapist]. My rage explodes further. One blast of rage-full energy to free me would never be enough.

The "smothering" within this safe workshop setting lasted for at least a half hour, although it seemed timeless. I used all of my formidable strength against a significant force, over and over and over. The continual freeing of myself utilizing my intense energy, and the continual re-smothering lasted until I was absolutely spent. Having utterly re-experienced the engulfing and smothering experience that had been my whole life, but NOW, having reacted and allowing my internal rage to grow and explode and to act in ways that I never would or was not allowed to if I was to survive.

I lay there spent on that mattress, on my back, no longer with a mattress covering me, and no longer experiencing myself as smothered internally for quite an extended time. I had a strange type of internal freedom. I felt clean. I felt separate. I somehow felt myself as a self by its' self. I lay there absorbing this experience. I knew I didn't have to do much to further incorporate it, nor do anything intentionally for it to have an effect on my life, but rather, for me to allow it to transform me with very little conscious effort on my part.

My foundation has changed. There may have been lingering emotional strings that I may have needed to finally cut, but my remembrance is that there were very few. I knew that I had started working this through before this workshop began. This intensive intervention was the finishing piece. This very concrete experience has freed me. I no longer felt smothered.

In terms of my life, my relationships dramatically shifted. I effortlessly connect with a very different type of woman, a more individuated person in their own right. The freedom of two more individuated persons being in relationship and the ease and effortlessness of that way of being together became spontaneously evident. With my clear "knowing" that it is from the intense and primal experiencing of buried emotional energies that one becomes free and transformed.

[This intervention depended on the two actors being psychologically connected to each other. He sensed that he could depend on me not to damage him, from his previous experiences with me. And I knew him well enough so that I was intuitively connected to him. When I have to act quickly in intense experiences, I must act intuitively—I don't have the time to *figure it out*. I used his words, "get the f* off of me" as his affirmation that what I was doing was right for him. I put myself on him with a mattress under me because I could give him the resistance he needed without overly personalizing my encounter with him. This made it easier for him to generalize this experience to his mother. Actually, we repeated his getting me off him three times, and this was enough for him to feel that it was endless. At the end of his statement he has the dramatic change in him due to his "intense and primal experiencing of buried emotional energies that one becomes free and transformed". [I agree with him about this. I would add that his experiencing was a full enough expression so that he finished and ended early traumas, which is deeply healing. In addition, when he goes deep into himself, to fully experience his mother's smothering of him, he evokes paradoxical change. Spontaneously, he changes so that he becomes more individuated. Since this is his change, he is able to own this change easily.]

See the schizoid patient's narrative for another example of Concretizing a Metaphor. Here, Thomas pulls a rope, or snake or demon out of his eye.

Dreaming While Awake

I very much value metaphors in ISP. The use of metaphor plays several important purposes. For example, earlier I talked about how metaphors often help to integrate a series of experiences. Here I want to present how *spontaneous* movement is used. As the person pays attention to their spontaneous movement, they are drawn into the depths of their body experience. This attention to their deeper body experiences leads them into *an altered state.* When this occurs, patients often describe their experiences as dream-like sequences. The process we use, in effect, treats them fully like they are dreams. We use the same processes that we employ to promote dream work. So here I am not only introducing you to dreaming while awake, I am also introducing you to dream-work generally in ISP.

First, the patient tells their dream. It is useful for the patient to tell the dream in the present tense. This can revivify the dream for him.

The patient is told that a dream is totally his production: that all people and animals and objects and all other features come from him and are his creation. Then the patient is asked to "own" each character in his dream. He says, *"the dog part of me"* is barking at me in an angry, menacing way. The patient is asked to consider that each character of a dream is *disowned* to the degree that each character is different from the patient. Therefore, the degree of difference for the male patient increases as the dream moves from a man to an old man to a woman, to a dog. The patient is invited to be each of these other characters, to express their feelings and to act in their ways.

Then the action is looked on as harboring a metaphor that the patient needs to intuit or interpret. For example, if the dream is about the patient being barked at in a menacing way by his dog, he may take this to mean that he is angry with himself, but he disowns these feelings. Then the therapist might have his patient role-play being the dog and expressing his anger at himself. Then the patient plays himself and responds to the dog part of him being angry with him and barking. What the patient becomes aware of is that he is angry with himself; as he plays the dog and then himself, he experiences why he is angry. He comes to the realization (for example) that he gave himself away to his parent(s). He gave into his parent(s)' insistence on how he should be. Then he may express his anger towards his parent(s) for coercing him. He can call them into the room and yell at them, or place them on a mattress opposite him and beat them. This work often fosters a deep integration of heart experiences, similar to what soft touch fosters.

The patient in Chapter 8, the phallic narcissist, dreamed of turning into an eagle that flew up high in the sky. He lived in the eagle part of himself soaring high in the sky. From looking into the dream he realized he needed to develop perspective about his life. Shifting his shape in the dream helped him to develop more clarity about himself*.

---

* Shape shifting is a Native-American experience, which is seen as a spiritual experience and a spiritual capability. This occurred in a patient who is strongly Christian. This dream experience greatly expanded his soulful experience of himself.

These two types of interventions presented so far in this section elicit experiences that the therapist cannot usually predict. This unpredictability emerges from patient interventions that greatly deepen his self-awareness. As this deepening occurs, the paradox of change is often evoked. The changes are spontaneous and emerge from deeper levels of the self, vs. change directed by the ego, which is often based on what a person should or wants to do.

Throughout the therapy the therapist asks her patient to pay attention to what is occurring in his body. This body focus is unusual and, again, often puts patients in an altered state. Suggestions that the patient see their mother or father from childhood, or that the patient's body wants to move, are more potent because of this altered state. The altered state has a broader range of attention (to body stimuli and to psychological experiences) and a lower level of resistance to suggestions. Notice that psychological content is not suggested; the patient is given opportunities that the person can use to go more deeply into their self. Again, ISP is primarily process focused. Dreaming While Awake and Concretizing Metaphors are interventions that I have developed.

If the therapist drives the content and the direction of the therapy, and therapy is very healing, then the therapist's sharpness is established. If the patient plays a major role in determining the content and direction of the therapy, then the patient's sharpness is established. Then the patient has the room in the therapy to gradually develop his self-awareness and therapeutic skills so that he can continue working himself on his own after he finishes his therapy.

The Stages of ISP

I see ISP as having two very general stages of psychotherapy. During the first stage, the patient does predominantly healing work, that is, reliving early traumas and finishing them, as we have described previously. During the second stage, the patient is involved in personal growth, self-development and spiritual expansion. The shift from one mode to the next is gradual.

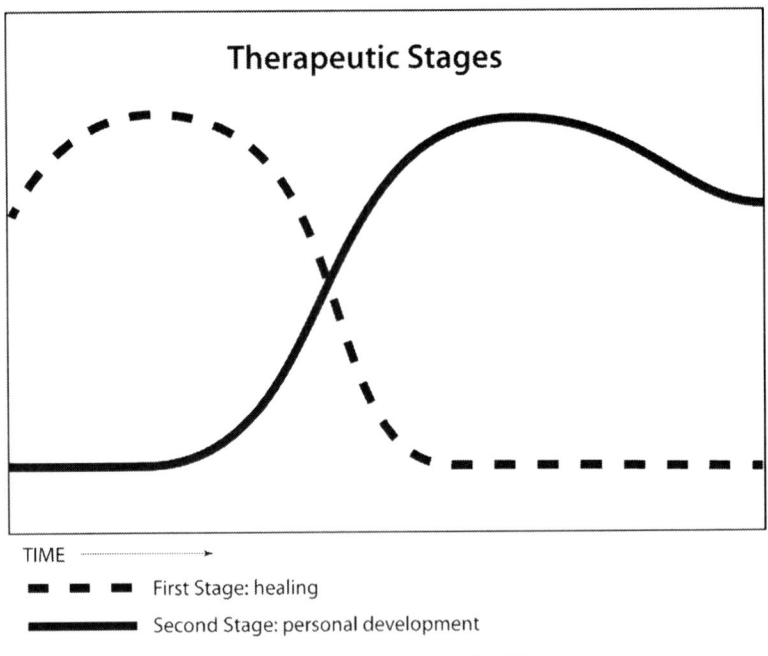

Therapeutic Stages

TIME →
- - - First Stage: healing
▬▬▬ Second Stage: personal development

The Two Stages of ISP

Illustration 14. The Two Stages of ISP

During the first stage of psychotherapy, the patient gradually builds up her courage one step at a time. Her courage enables her to work on her self-development. She deals with the character- shaping traumas she has experienced. She does this by regressing and reliving the traumas and finishing them. As she does this, she also works on externalizing her parental introjects so she becomes more fully her self.

By the time she reaches the second stage of her therapy, she realizes that she has the resources to explore the deepest levels of her self.

Exploring spirituality in ISP requires taking leaps into our depths without knowing what we will encounter. This process bears repeating. This endeavor requires a high degree of courage to deal with the risks. We do not expect patients to take these leaps without helping them to prepare. Remember that a major, repeating ISP process is the Awareness Cycle that I explicated earlier in this book. Each cycle ends in its fourth step: Self-appreciation for having taken the risks to move through the prior three steps, which requires dealing with unanticipated aspects of self that emerge spontaneously. As one repeatedly goes through the Awareness Cycle, there is a progression of going deeper into the Self. So patients *gradually increase their courage* to proceed during the course of their psychotherapy.

Going deeper into the self eventuates (if a patient chooses to stay in ISP long enough) in encountering their Soul. I see the soul as the deepest core of the self. Physically, this is a movement down into an awareness of one's deep belly and pelvis. Eastern philosophy and religion name this body area the *Hara*. The soul is the pattern of deep beliefs, awareness and knowledge of one's core self.

In the soul, we expand our feeling of connection to human beings and living creatures. We also feel connected to the "divine." *As we live in our soul, we move more gracefully through the world.*

The *energy* connected to the soul's pattern is called the *spirit*. As we descend into our soul, we gain access to more and more of our energy. As we descend into our soul, we gain access to much greater streams of our energy and to a much fuller realization of our deepest resources. This often makes our arduous journey worthwhile!

Not every patient chooses to go this far in exploring her soul and spirit. As therapists, we learn to accept that this is an important right of patients. Patients experience their souls differently from each other, and we must accept this, too. There is no one established pattern of soul.

CHAPTER 10

Moving Towards the End of the Psychotherapy

Introduction

During the first stage of ISP, the patient's work on their early past, finishing this work and reducing their armoring, leads to their increased self-awareness in the here and now. Self-awareness increases during their work in the second stage. This puts the patient in the position of increasingly playing a more active role in shaping the therapy. If you are more aware of feeling pain in a part of your body then you can suggest where to work and, perhaps, even what kind of work you need to do. Effective therapists pay careful attention to these patient inclinations and suggestions.

These inclinations and suggestions gradually increase during the second stage of ISP as de-armoring continues and patients gain more access to their intuitive processes. Patient access to their intuition increases during the second phase as they increase contact with their core self and soul. Patients grow to have more trust in their intuitive processes because using them has desirable effects.

Forgiveness

After the patient has gone through much therapeutic work, such as experiencing and expressing unconscious feelings of anger, sadness and love towards primary figures, usually parents, *perhaps the patient is ready to deal with forgiveness.* What they truly need is to deal with the internalized mother and father parts of themselves. They need to discover and vent these held-in, unconscious feelings as they externalize these parental introjects. It takes courage—the capacity to do what they need to do with their parental parts in spite of feeling anxious, scared or even terrified. When they make the choice to proceed to express their feelings, they are not aware of the extent of these feelings. Full awareness only comes to us as we finish with experiencing and expressing what was felt as we were traumatized in childhood. What we can do is proceed gradually in small steps, and this gives us the opportunity to gradually build up our courage.

As our courage grows, eventually we realize that we have the capacity to deal with the depths of our inner life. *So the development of courage is a cornerstone for deep inner exploration in ISP.* Increasing the grounding of patients is another way to support patients to move into their inner work because this gives them the stability they need to proceed. Grounding is enhanced during the first stage of ISP directly from doing stress work, and from loosening up the muscles of the legs.

After dealing with the traumas of their earlier years, patients may get to the place where they are ready and able to forgive important figures in their life. If you choose to forgive someone in your life, you are not absolving the person (others or yourself) for his or her misdeeds. You cannot alter that past reality now! The degree to which you are tied into your past is reduced by your act of forgiveness. You promote a fuller closure with your self and your introjects so that you can move on with your life. After forgiving, you still have the choice to alter your interpersonal relationship to the person or not. If you choose not to alter your relationship with others, then you cannot expect anything new from them. What is important is the shift inside of you.

Patients may undercut finishing their feeling work by bringing to the fore other powerful feelings on which to focus. Patients may shift from doing all of their anger and mourning work by concentrating on feelings of love or understanding of primary figures. Patients can also reduce the full expression of their feelings by using guilt or anxiety to undercut their more interactive feelings. Forgiveness is the cap to finishing the expression of these more interactive feelings.

A Matrix of Forgiveness

	To Self	To Others
Done to Me	I Have Hurt Me	Others Have Hurt Me
I Have Done	I Have Hurt Me	I Have Hurt Others

A Matrix of Forgiveness

Illustration 15. A Matrix of Forgiveness

Completing the expression of feelings to their parental introjects or others, followed by their forgiveness of them, leads the forgiver to have a deep release followed by exhaustion and a feeling of relief. It is important to explore how the patient feels about their parents after they express their forgiveness so that they express it publicly in front of their therapist. They may have a major shift in their feelings towards them from their act of forgiving. It is important for the patient to realize this shift in themselves because this may herald a major change in their relationship with their parent. If the patient is forgiving himself, he is more likely to have major alterations in his feelings towards himself. It is crucial for the patient to realize this shift in order to complete his consolidation of his more evolved self.

A way for the therapist to proceed in this area is to ask the patient if they are ready to forgive the other person now. This is an attempt to have the patient check himself out to see if this readiness is true for him. If the patient says no, then the therapist accepts this and the work proceeds to other relevant areas. If the patient recognizes that they are ready to forgive, then the therapist supports this process. The patient is asked to invoke the presence of their parent or whomever else the patient wishes to forgive, to express their feelings. After these feelings are expressed fully, it is important for the therapist to tell the patient that they still have the choice to express their forgiveness to the person directly in their life or not.

The therapist then proceeds to asking the patient if they feel differently about the person now.

> <u>A Patient Narrative of Forgiveness</u>—In our treatment, there were several instances where I came to forgive myself and/or others after having surfaced both anger and sadness that had been locked away (out of safety by my subconscious).

I recalled two events where my mother 'forgot' me. My mother took care of five of us (I was the youngest) mostly as a single parent. The first was when I had just turned 5 years old. I was wandering around the sports section of a department store and I became disconnected from my brother and three sisters. My mother was late for an appointment and as soon as she checked out, she piled everyone in the car as quickly as she could. It wasn't until she arrived home and they were piling out of the car that she realized I wasn't in the car.

She was horrified. An assistant manager had found me and took me up to the manager's office where I waited. She quickly came back to find me worried that I wasn't ever going to go back home again and I didn't know why.

In our session, I recall the bodywork agitating that memory—reproducing the feeling that I was excess baggage, disposable, and not valued. I spent that session confronting my mother. Asking her why she forgot me and *forgiving myself for believing it was my fault she had the burden of having a 5th child.* I wasn't supposed to be here. She was on the pill when she had me. I was a "mistake". *I forgave myself for believing all my life that I was a burden, extra baggage or an eye sore. I spent most of my life trying to prove that I matter.* [The italics is to emphasize his forgiveness. This is an example of the patient forgiving himself.]

The second instance was when my mother (with one car) was working two jobs supporting 5 children who were either working as teenagers or in school activities.

I was 11. It was late November after basketball practice (after 7:30 PM). The principal, coaches and even the janitors were all leaving the building. It was before the convenience of the mobile phone, so I assured them that my mother would be minutes away—again, not wanting to be a burden to their busy lives. After repeatedly asking me if I was ok standing in the parking lot. I insisted that they leave and that I would be all right. It was below freezing as I stood and moved around the parking lot trying to keep myself warm. 7:30 became 8:00 became 9:00 and 9:00 became 9:30. The cold had penetrated my soul. In those two hours, I went through anger, sadness, fear, but most of all shame. I was ashamed that I was left alone to freeze. That's how much I didn't matter in the world. I was certain I was going to die. My mother arrived worried sick about me. I was quiet; my fingers were purple and were no longer tingling. In therapy, contorting my body and engaging in the breathing techniques re-created that cold moment where I was shivering, alone and abandoned.

I confronted my mother again. However, this time I was torn between anger and empathy. My mother's circumstances were not 'controllable' by her, given everything in life that was thrown at her at once (my father abandoning her, her trying to make ends meet, and providing the basics of food, clothes, and an education). I wanted to forgive her but I first had to work through my anger at her for leaving a little kid to wait 2 hours in the freezing cold.

I accessed that memory and needed to work through what was buried underneath a façade of self-protection. That little kid felt like no one cared about him. He was on his own—protective of himself and his heart. I didn't have the opportunity to tell my mother in those actual moments that I felt abandoned and that I also felt like I didn't matter. In the safety of the therapy, I recreated another opportunity to speak to my mother, tell her how hard supporting five children all by herself seemed to me now as an adult and forgave her for being late to pick me up.

I also realized that in both cases that I failed to show up for myself and how that is a theme that cuts across my relationships.

Gratitude

Here is an example of gratitude from me: I feel intense gratitude about being healthy, being able to exercise regularly and to work creatively presenting the ISP approach.

I prefer to work on gratitude with patients during the second stage of their ISP therapy. During the second stage individuals are becoming more expansive in their lives as they explore their core selves and then their souls. They focus more on their current lives. During the first stage, they have worked on their past as they deal with their unfinished trauma from their early years. Finishing the traumas leads to their resolution. As more traumas are resolved, patients gradually increase their grounding in their present lives. This grounding forms the foundation for the second stage's work.

It is not that I won't work gratitude, which is expressed spontaneously, during the first stage of therapy. If the patient introduces it spontaneously, I will, but *I won't work expansively with the process of gratitude.* I hold off for the second stage to help patients bring gratitude as a practice into their lives. And if patients don't introduce gratitude spontaneously during this second stage, I may introduce it at as a possibility, as an ongoing practice in their lives.

What is feeling gratitude? – It is recognition of the gifts that a person has gotten in their life, without being required to reciprocate by giving gifts back. Expressing gratitude opens the person's heart and mind to the blessings and learning that have come their way.

Gratitude is the person's appreciation for what they have received. Feeling gratitude for receiving gifts promotes experiencing deep comfort and times of intense inner peace. Giving gratitude comes from our getting much out of life and living, which is true for many without their being aware that this is so. We get blessings and learnings from others or from the lessons inherent in living our lives.

Gratitude also prompts us to give to others without expecting anything in return. Our giving is often done anonymously, such as, giving money to charities that help to care for the poor or sick. So gratitude leads to cycles of deeply feeling gifted, which opens one's heart, and eventuates in giving to others in heart-felt ways. This cycle provides deep support to one's life. And this deep support promotes a deep exploration of a person's soul.

Previously in this book I talked about the importance of gradually developing more courage to risk having contact with our souls. Now we add to this the deep blessings we receive from contacting our gratitude, which also leads to us to living our lives more deeply. These are two potent and important processes that support us to explore our depths.

Gratitude and Addictions (Arrien 2009) – Gratitude helps people to go beyond the addictions that they acquired in their life. And gratitude is very useful in transcending addictions that may be acquired by engaging in ISP.

One addiction is the fixation on what is not working in a person's life. Therapy often proceeds by focusing on the problems in a person's life, especially during the first stage of ISP. On the other hand, gratitude strongly brings the focus to what is working in the person's life. Gratitude develops a generosity of spirit toward oneself and their life; this fosters the gift of perspective where people see more of the totality of their lives. They see what works and what doesn't work. This dilutes the addiction to seeing themselves as not living fully and successfully.

Gratitude also helps to transcend the addiction to seek great emotional intensity. This grows out of an exaggerated fear that life is dull, boring, too routine, and not very meaningful. People with this addiction dramatize their lives; they blow their lives up out of proportion to get more intense experiences. Feeling gratitude increases their awareness of the blessings that already exist in their lives. They are helped to become aware of the fullness in their lives now that exists independently of intense emotionality. I focus on this addiction because ISP sessions often include the expression of intense emotions that accompany the finishing of childhood trauma during the first stage of ISP.

Since feeling gratitude plays an important role in reducing, or even eliminating, addictions that are reinforced during the first stage of ISP, I promote the gratitude process in patients during the second stage.

Gratitude Benefits Four Areas of Life:

1. Personal Benefits. Expressing gratitude reduces people's stress and anxiety levels. At the same time it increases their feelings

of well-being and happiness. Also the quality of their rest and sleep increases, which helps to replenish them.
2. Work Benefits. Expressing gratitude to others by leaders, managers and workers engenders increased cooperation, creativity and productivity of all employees. The quality and quantity of work productivity may increase.
3. Relationship Benefits. Gratitude, given freely, fosters increased generosity and reciprocity between people. Mutual trust increases. And this helps peoples' hearts to be more open to each other.
4. Spiritual Benefits. Gratitude helps people to have increasing contact with their core self, and their soul.

It should be more obvious that the experience of gratitude plays an important healing factor in the process of ISP psychotherapy.

Patient Narrative about Gratitude

I experience gratitude when I feel a sense of accepting all of my self in the world at the present moment.

Another Patient Narrative about Gratitude

I'm grateful for the body psychotherapy process in that it has allowed me to connect with a much deeper and genuine part of my true self, and thus "allowed me to just be rather than try so hard." In just being I have spontaneously created a satisfying and fairly effortless existence and comfortable life.

Jerry Perlmutter, PhD

Terminating Psychotherapy

When I talk of termination in this context I refer to saying goodbye to persons we have been very close to. Patients are moving on because the treatment relationship is being ended. The closer they have been to the therapist they are leaving, and therapy is usually a very intimate relationship, the greater the learning potential of the termination.

The difficulty of termination with a therapist that they are close to is that the sad feelings will be intense. Some patients deal with terminations by abruptly leaving without signaling their intent so that they can avoid their pain. It is very useful for a therapist to contact their patient and ask them to come in for sessions to deal with their termination. Terminations are crises. The Chinese language characters for crisis are danger and opportunity. This sums up a key aspect of what I said just above.

Patients who run away from saying goodbye to their therapist often deal with the important terminations in their life in this same manner. In life, avoiding the impact of leave-taking may take the form of not showing up for goodbye parties, or not informing friends that they are leaving or moving. If their friends know they are leaving, they still may avoid talking about their departure. They may take distracting vacations. Or they may take anti-depressants. They may avoid being intimate with others so that the pain of saying goodbye is truncated. What I am trying to demonstrate is that how a person says goodbye is an important clue to how they live their lives. The termination with their therapist is an opportunity for the patient to see how they live, and to make changes in their lifestyle to increase the satisfaction and meaningfulness of their lives.

It is useful to identify the components of a full termination so that we can help mourners to have greater learning from this process. This approach to termination helps the patient to do important work right up to end of their time in therapy. I have used a mnemonic device called the "5 Rs" of termination that I use at the end of therapy.

Terminations are times when there is a great tendency to be introspective. People need to expand this tendency so that they review (R1) the full swath of the relationship they are ending. As they do this review, they reevaluate (R2) the relationship, and, in particular, their role in the relationship. A primary emotion of termination is remorse (R3). (I use the term remorse instead of sadness for memory purposes only.) One of the major sources of remorse I call *the "gap" which refers to the loss of the person in our lives.* Some people experience an accompanying physical space in their bodies. All terminations include remorse from a gap. The intensity of this feeling is directly dependent on how close we have been to the person we are departing from. The closer the relationship, the stronger we feel remorse from the gap.

The second source of remorse stems from *the guilt or shame that stems from not living up to our personal standards in the relationship.* We did, said or felt things that were departures from our moral code.

A third source of remorse stems from *the experience of incompleteness.* Here we put off expressing thoughts and feelings, or doing things because we assumed that there was no rush, and at a deeper level, that we have forever.

These three sources of remorse are additive and determine the intensity of remorse at termination. The stronger their remorse, the longer and deeper they must mourn. Mourning fully fosters finishing their termination and moving on with their life.

It is important that we normalize these feelings of remorse or sadness; that we assure patients that feeling strong feelings of sadness at the termination of therapy are customary and that they are not *depressed.*

We need to mourn, to feel the sadness and pain of ending fully in order to move on with our living. There are strong societal beliefs that it is not okay to feel sadness or emotional pain; that experiencing these feelings weaken us, injure us psychologically. These beliefs have been repeatedly challenged in ISP therapy. So at termination, the patient has one last opportunity to learn and incorporate that societal norms that *challenge* experiencing one's pain or mourning are not a path to healthy living. This is particularly true because *incomplete mourning* is a path to depression.

Having patients review their sources of remorse (R3), helps them to review how they live their lives, e.g., have they been avoiding being close to others to limit their sadness--do they start terminating relationships from the start by not allowing themselves to be very intimate? Do they act as if they have a lot of time so that they delay and delay staying current with the person in the relationship? As a patient takes this deeper look at their sources of remorse, they get a much fuller awareness of themselves. This deep self-awareness may initiate the "paradox of change." Now the patient may be impelled to spontaneously change or they may create plans for personal change (the latter is ego directed change). Of course they can do both.

Regression (R4) is the next "R". At ending times, we tend to think, feel and act like we did earlier in the therapeutic relationship. In therapeutic situations this *regression* can be disconcerting to patients and professionals alike. We may lead ourselves to question the efficacy of our efforts. When regression is seen as usual and accepted (this is a process of normalization, too), then instead of feeling demoralized, the effects can be developmental. The patient can take this opportunity to "go back" to deal with and further resolve earlier conflicts or impasses in their relationship with their therapist or with other people who are primary, such as parents and spouses.

Healing Body, Self and Soul

If we learn our lessons from mourning fully, and we develop the capacity to live life more fully, more meaningfully than before, then the last R ensues…rebirth (R5). Rebirth occurs when the rich opportunities of mourning are utilized and we experience this latest transformation in our lives at the end of our therapy.

I invite you to use this termination model to identify more fully your style of living in the world. And then you can evaluate your style. You may develop a plan to alter your style so that it becomes more fulfilling and congruent with your deeper self. Then you may experience a transformative rebirth experience.

For those who want to do the self-analysis, start by identifying an important person you have terminated with because they have died, or you have divorced them, or they or you have moved away. Take notes. As you picture this person, breathe deeply, and notice if you feel the sadness of a gap in your life from missing this person… Are there discontinuities in this gap? For example, is this a person whom you would expect intense gap feelings because they are your parent, or a spouse or a close friend. On review, do you find yourself not allowing yourself to develop strong or very intimate feelings? Have you avoided the pain of feeling a gap? Evaluate your behavior and decide if you want to be more intimate in closer relationships even if separating then causes you more pain. Create a plan for using this data so that you feel more satisfied and authentic, if this is relevant to you.

Observe this experience of separation again while breathing deeply to see if you faced the termination fully or not. If you did not face the termination fully, notice what you did to avoid the ending. Use the text above on termination to look at examples of avoidance tactics. Identify what you want to do differently in the future.

Then look at your feelings about terminating with this person. See if you left the relationship feeling incomplete. Do you feel sad because there were things you needed to say, or do and that you didn't? Did you tell yourself that what you needed to say could wait, until it was too late to do so? Would you try to stay more current with important others in your life in the future? Write a plan to do so.

Then review your feelings and your relationship to see if you feel guilt or shame, because you did something in the relationship that did not fit with your moral and ethical codes. Maybe you need to change your code. Alternately, maybe you need to live more morally and ethically? Spell out your answer. Be specific, what will you do differently in the future?

Notice the variety of goals and actions you are planning to implement in the future. Notice how you feel, given these newly developed plans to alter your current life. Keep tracking your reactions as you implement your new behavior. You may want to re-plan based upon some of the impact of your new behavior.

My Termination with this Book

I have enjoyed the process of writing this book, because I felt I was being creative while shaping this manuscript. I had one time when I was considering bailing out of writing and publishing, but I consulted a friend here in the retirement community in which I live now. He helped me to face and resolve a double bind I had put myself into. So I proceeded to finish the manuscript.

Because the psychotherapy approach I developed and this book have flowed out of me, I have continually been transformed as I wrote it. As I wrote, I clarified for myself what I have been doing and why I have been doing it. My career as an ISP practitioner has enriched me.

Healing Body, Self and Soul

It has been a wonderful journey to work doing what I love for forty years. And I have extended my career by four years by writing this book. I am uncertain about how it will be received by others, and I am confortable with taking this risk and seeing what happens. Thank you so much for taking this journey with me by reading this book.

{If you wish to contact me about this book and your reading experience, email me at <u>ispbook@yahoo.com</u>.}

BIBLIOGRAPHY

Arrien, A. (2009). *Gratitude: The Essential Practice for Happiness and Fulfillment.* Louisville, Colorado: Sounds True [CD].

Brenner, C. (1955). *An Elementary Textbook of Psychoanalysis.* Garden City, New York: Doubleday Anchor Books.

Brown, M. (undated). *The Healing Touch: An Introduction to Organismic Psychotherapy.* Self-published.

Johanson, G. and Kurz, R. (1991). *Grace Unfolding: Psychotherapy in the Spirit of the Tao-te Ching.* New York: Bell Tower.

Johnson, S.M. (1985). *Characterological Transformation: The Hard Work Miracle.* New York: W.W. Norton & Company.

Johnson, S.M. (1987). *Humanizing the Narcissistic Style.* New York: WW Norton & Company.

Jung, C.G. (1964). *Man and His Symbols.* London: Aldus Books Limited.

Kurz, R. (1990). *Body-Centered Psychotherapy: The Hakomi Method.* Mendocino, California: LifeRhythm.

Lesowitz, N and Sammons, M.B. (2011). *Gratitude Power Workbook.* Berkeley, California: Cleis Press Inc.

Lowen, A. (1958). *The Language of the Body.* New York: Macmillan Publishing Company.

Lowen, A. (1990). *The Spirituality of the Body.* New York: Macmillan Publishing Company.

Lowen, A. and Lowen, L. (1977). *The Way to Vibrant Health: A Manual of Biogenetic Exercises.* New York: Harper & Row, Publishers.

Mahler, M.S. (1968). *On Human Symbiosis and the Vicissitudes of Individuation.* New York: International Universities Press.

Mahler, M.S. (1972). *Rapprochement Subphase of the Separation –Individuation Process.* Psychoanalytic Quarterly, 41, 487-506.

Mahler, M.S., Pine, R. and Bergman, A. (1975). *The Psychological Birth of the Human Infant.* New York: Basic Books.

Mix, P.J. (2006, Sept.). *A Monumental Legacy: The Unique and Unheralded Contributions of John and Joyce Weir to the Human Development Field.* The Journal of Applied Behavioral Science, pp. 276-299.

Perlmutter, J. (2010, revised edit.) *Using Integrative Somatic Psychotherapy to Heal PTSD and Dissociation: An Overview.* Arlington Hts, IL: Midwest Institute for Somatic Psychotherapy.

Perls, F.S. (1992). *Gestalt Therapy Verbatim.* Highland, New York: The Gestalt Journal.

Pert, C.B. (1997). *Molecules of Emotion: Why You Feel the Way You Feel.* New York: Scribner Press.

Pierrakos, J.C. (1990). *Core Energetics: Developing the Capacity to Love and Heal.* Mendocino, California: LifeRhythm.

Reich, W. (1972, 3rd. edit.). *Character Analysis.* New York: Farrar, Straus and Giroux.

Reich, W. (1973). *The Function of the Orgasm: Sex-Economic Problems of Biological Energy.* New York: Simon and Schuster.

Winnicot, D.W. (1965). *The Maturational Processes and the Facilitating Environment.* New York: International University Press.

JERRY PERLMUTTER, PHD, PROFESSIONAL ACTIVITIES

Body Psychotherapist, Workshop Leader and Trainer

I have conducted a private practice in body psychotherapy from 1970 to 2010 in the greater Chicago area. After working for about 15 years, I realized that the way I worked differed greatly from the persons I had trained with: Alan Richardson, PhD, Malcolm Brown, PhD and Alexander Lowen, MD. Formulating my approach became very important to me as I started training persons to do body psychotherapy. I named my work Integrative Body Psychotherapy (ISP).

I have also led a variety of workshops in the area of body psychotherapy. One of my primary efforts was an annual, seven-day residential workshop done at George Williams College, Lake Geneva, Wisconsin. It was amicably called the SoulWork-Shop. Its full name was Body, Self and Soul—in Motion. My staff and I did over thirty of these workshops. It combined many approaches into a cohesive workshop design: Yoga, expressive movement, breathwork, shamanic methods, transference work, and intense body touch work done in trios of participants. Participants highly rated their experiences.

In 1997 I was a founder of the Midwest Institute in Somatic Psychotherapy (MISP). This non-profit organization was designed to promote ISP and to be a professional organization for trained body psychotherapists. I was an Executive Director and a Fellow of MISP.

Five years ago, I retired from my psychotherapy private practice. I moved to Durham, North Carolina.

Dr. Perlmutter can be contacted at: ispbook@yahoo.com.